The Book of the Sun

Praise from Other People

"This book powerfully conveys an extraordinarily significant series of messages for our turbulent times of evolutionary transition, including that the intrinsic oneness of life and mind as expressed by the Cosmic Intelligence of the Sun whereby we are in fact each other and need to act accordingly. The engaging inner conversations range across all the big questions in a simple and accessible style. Real progress is towards Light and Love, but without forgetting the reality of pain and the refreshment of laughter. A genuine revelation."

David Lorimer, MA, PGCE, FRSA, writer, lecturer, editor, Programme Director - The Scientific and Medical Network, author and editor of many books, France

This is an astonishing book. Jenny Rook is an experienced writer and her book is an easy read. But its contents are enormously important for us and our planet. Jenny has a direct connection to the Sun, which tells her that it is the master intelligence of our solar system. It points out that our Earth is very special and that all who come here have a duty to learn to love.

This is an exceptional book. It has been channelled from the highest consciousness in our planetary system, the Sun. It describes the structure of the cosmos; the roles all the planets play; who we are on this Earth; and the process we have to go through while we are here. The Sun tells us the world is going through a very traumatic situation as those people on our planet are moving from the third to the fourth degree of consciousness. This will be an enormous change in our experience and understanding. It is a mind-stretching read which I highly recommend.

Dr Peter Fenwick - internationally renowned neuropsychiatrist, Fellow of the UK Royal College of Psychiatrists, President of the British branch of The International Association for Near-Death Studies, with appointments at the Maudsley Hospital, the John Radcliffe Hospital and the Broadmoor Special Hospital for Violent Offenders

"Jenny's story is fascinating and engaging; spanning from committed atheist and materialist; to experiences of intimate mystical communion with the sun. Her accounts of this communion speak to the heart of spirit, service, and love. They shine a light on the underlying love and unity in our universe and offer a divine context for our journey here on Earth."

Austin Bridges, Assistant Director of L/L Research, Louisville, Kentucky

"Reading this book is like basking in the warmth and richness of the sun. The words are like rays of light that glisten on our soul and you realise that within this world no one is truly alone. In fact, we are all connected because the sun connects us all though each season, to each other, wherever we are in the world. The words written through Jenny show us that we are interconnected not isolated. Such hope, such wisdom that has reached us at the perfect time."

Anna Kälin, Child and Adolescent Psychoanalytical Psychotherapist, Bristol, UK

"Jenny writes with a lightness and iridescence that carries deep wisdom and surety. I loved the truth of her words, feeling the resonance, the recognition and the reassurance all conveyed so exquisitely. This is a book for our times; it will meet and nourish the many who seek a new paradigm of understanding for their soul's journey."

Katy Nicol, therapist, Stroud, UK

"Who is Jenny? The Sun says she is one with everything that is, was, and ever will be; one with infinite intelligence and creativity on its playful journey through aeons of cosmic progression back to Source. Jenny Rook's provocative dialogue with the Sun/herself/all encapsulates her jolt out of decades of material atheism into the gnosis of divine light and infinite love. Her joy is palpable. Her experience shared as fact or parable enables me to trust my own, including that:

- we are greatly loved and cared for by divine essence no matter what;

- time as we know it does not exist;
- death releases the spirit to the loving care of those gone before;
- the manner of our death and birth, the people we meet, all is pre-ordered, including the free will to grow or not, and;
- love, compassion, forgiveness, empathy is all there is."

Judith Crichton, PhD formerly Vice President, Prudential of America, Toronto, Canada

"The Book of Sun is a powerful work that bridges both sides of the delicate membrane that separates the imaginary from the imaginal. It was wonderful to see Jenny Rook's evolution through so many different domains. She is indeed a complex person: atheist and esotericist, mother and child, psychoanalyst and prophet.

Jeffrey Mishlove, Winner of the Bigelow Prize for the best essay giving proof of life after death, interviewer and doctor of parapsychology, USA

"When undertaking an intense programme of meditation, Jenny Rook experienced a profound sense of love, light, joy and compassion that seemed to come from beyond her own consciousness – from the universe itself. As she went deeper into this awakening state, she became open to words of wisdom and insight, which explain the spiritual nature of our solar system, our galaxy and ultimately the cosmos as a whole. In *The Book of the Sun*, Jenny shares these insights, providing an optimistic view that our lives are really filled with love and light and by using techniques to see through the veil of the third dimension, we can live together with kindness and compassion, with beauty and with truth. The cosmic, spiritual teachings in *The Book of the Sun* are underpinned by practical examples from Jenny's personal life and her extensive experience as a psychoanalyst supporting children and young people towards mental wellbeing."

Christine Heron, writer, Glastonbury, UK

"*The Book of the Sun* is a truly fascinating read, both profound in its wisdom, and also challenging and thought-provoking at times. It can allow expansion of consciousness, while at the same time creating an extraordinary empathy with the whole of the human condition. It left me wanting more... "

Joanna Casey, artist, Stroud, UK

The Book of the Sun

by

Jenny Rook

"A powerful work that bridges both sides of the delicate membrane that separates the imaginary from the imaginal."

Jeffrey Mishlove, Winner of the Bigelow Prize for the best essay giving proof of life after death, interviewer and doctor of parapsychology, USA

"This book contains the core truths of the universe. I recommend you read it."

Richard Rudd, author, poet, mystic, creator of the Gene Keys, Devon UK

ISBN: 979-8-9861057-9-6

10 9 8 7 6 5 4 3 2 1

This book is typeset in Californian FB with Bahnschrift SemiBold SemiCondensed used as the display typeface.

Publisher Imprint: Serapis Bey Publishing

Literary agent and editor: Wendy Yorke

Front cover image and book design: Natasa Ivancevic

First printing edition 2022

Dedication

To Oscar, with love

About the Author

Jenny Rook was born in Essex, UK and educated at York University, where she graduated with a degree in English and Music. Studying the greats of literature called a halt to her burgeoning desire to write. After various adventures in: the scrap trade; bookselling; helping run an employment agency; and having children, she settled back into her first love, writing. Her first fiction book *Fly By Night* (1989) was accepted by Headline, the first publisher she sent it to. This was the first of a fantasy trilogy and Headline wanted all three. All her fiction books are published under the name Jenny Jones. Two adult ghost novels followed, *Where the Children Cry* (1998) and *The Blue Manor* (1995) both published by Gollancz. Five other fantasy/horror books for teenagers were published by Scholastic (1994, 1995, 1997), Hodder (1995) and Orion (2000).

In 2006, Jenny qualified as a psychoanalytic psychotherapist for children and their families. She worked mainly for the NHS and also volunteered for Sure Start (a UK government initiative to help with the early stages in a mother and baby's relationship), before taking early retirement to look after her elderly mother. Jenny now lives with her husband, mother, and three dogs in the Cotswolds and writes nonfiction.

Contents

Foreword

by Dr Peter Fenwick MB BChir (Cantab) DPM FRCPsych

If I was to tell you that this book was dictated to the author by the sun, you would probably put it straight back on the shelf. Don't. It is very well written, easy to read and contains a raft of ideas that will keep you afloat for a long time. Jenny Rook was brought up in a family of committed atheists. She has been a committed atheist herself since, at the age of eight, she asked her father if he believed in God and he replied that there was no evidence for such belief.

She trained for six years as a child psychoanalytical psychotherapist. About three years ago she decided to take a web-based Finder's course, produced by a Harvard-trained psychologist Dr Jeffery Martin. It was designed to induce non-duality, in other words, to change your consciousness so that you and the world become one thing. About 70% of the people who take the course have an alteration in consciousness which in some people can progress to the level experienced by the Christian mystics. Jenny was one of the successful ones. Her ego – her sense of "I" - began to crumble and she entered a state of ecstasy which, with varying intensity, has been with her ever since.

It was while she was in this state that she felt one day that the Sun was talking to her, describing the cosmos and the sun's position as the major creative consciousness in our solar system. And telling her that she was to give a message to humanity.

Her response was, Why Me? Because you will not make a religion of it was the reply!

With the appearance of the sun, Jenny was in ecstasy, filled with light and love. At times Jenny asked the Sun, Why? It replied *You are Me and I am You. 'I am' is you without the impermanent furniture of the mind, all those parts of you which are transient: your memories, sensations, emotions, perceptions, thoughts, feeling. Everything changes. It's all transient, and your thoughts are the most transient thing of all. On this planet are all the people that have lived here throughout the incarnation of your world. If you look around, you will see that they are all you, and experience the sense of family. Why do we come to this world? To learn to love. When one has learnt enough then one can go to another dimension. You see, everything exists in My mind and imagination. In Me you see the incandescent nuclear reactor, whilst I am boundless consciousness, stretching through the universe into galaxies and times that you cannot know now.*

But why do people come here if they are going to suffer? *To learn the hard lesson of learning to love. You see this planet is a third density planet. The first density is of rock the second density of biology, plants and animals, and the third is all humanity; we are all part of this wonderful cosmic dance. Our planet is one of the most beautiful in our galaxy, and as you move and your consciousness changes more into love, humanity moves from the third to the fourth density, where everything is the vibration of love. Another time line is now arising, where everything is seen as material. If that progresses it will lead to the destruction of our species. I come from the supreme, final source, source is within Me and within you.* When Jenny asks about suffering, the Sun points out that it arises from deep within us and that it can be transmuted by the essence of love.

At times you can see Jenny's training as a child analyst coming through. Your behaviour depends on how you were brought up, If you had no parental love, you have no love to give. But you can, the Sun adds, always go round and try again in another life. Emotion changes: in misery a kind word may alter the feeling. In joy, a sad news item may bring you down. Your perceptions change as you look around you, your sensations change as you step into a cold shower. It's all transient, and your thoughts are the most transient thing of all.

There are lovely quotes which are pure expressions of Jenny. She has read Nagel's paper, 'What is it like to be a bat?' which threw the materialistic world into a quandary, and the Sun points out that Jenny might as well ask, What is it like to be a cake? You can name every ingredient but you will never know what taste someone else experiences when they eat it. So it is with all others, except what you meet in love. And then you understand.

There is much more in this book about the Sun, about why human behaviour is like it is, why the world is constructed in such a way that there is widespread expression of love if you want it. You will be pleased to hear that the Sun told Jenny we will all get there in the end, but that this thinking is veiled from us in our third dimension.

The great psychoanalyst Wilfred Bion said that the answer is the death of the question. The Sun works through Jenny's knowledge of analysis and tackles some of the most fundamental questions. As a psychoanalytical psychotherapist Jenny knows all about the tricks the mind can play. But she denies that these experiences are self-generated mind tricks. And when she describes how she integrates what she has learned from her own experiences into her work, it shows clearly that her messages from the Sun are of infinite value.

Solar deities such as the Roman Apollo, Greek Helios and the Nordic Goddess Sol have been the focus of religions in many cultures throughout most of recorded history, usually reflecting the sun's perceived power and strength. Jenny's Sun is very different, neither male nor female. It tells us that our planet is the most beautiful and tender of all the planets and that people come to it for a life in which they learn how to love. It teaches us the importance of love, of kindness and forgiveness – for ourselves as well as others. It is pure love and it spreads this love endlessly throughout the Cosmos. What we really are is love, and it is realising this that will enable us to live more happily.

Music Master

... Watch the dust grains moving
In the light near the window.
Their dance is our dance.
We rarely hear the inward music,
but we're all dancing to it nevertheless,
directed by the one who teaches us,
the pure joy of the sun,
our music master.

Rumi

Introduction

This book is the record of an extraordinary experience I had, which took place during the first year of the Covid pandemic. In the next few pages there is a brief autobiography, setting the scene for this strange and life-changing event, that might also go some way towards explaining it. For the mystery of who we are is profound, and this background is part of my understanding about what happened.

*****

At the age of eight, I asked my father if he believed in God.

'No evidence, dear,' he said. 'No evidence at all.'

This became my position, sternly rationalist, convinced that all religion, to paraphrase, was bunk. Nevertheless the little girl, who had always loved her fairy stories, was always curious about history and mythology, and the way they intertwined. Why did people believe these things when there was really no evidence? I became fascinated by the ancient Egyptians, their exotic mythology and their strange ideas about reincarnation. My father had several glossy books about the pyramids and the Valley of the Kings. We went on a school trip to see the Tutankhamun exhibition and that beautiful golden face haunted my dreams for years. Dad had other books about the Ancient Sun Kingdoms of

Central and South America, the Aztecs, Maya and Inca, and I devoured these too. But I knew this was all ancient mythology, even more adrift than our current day Christianity. It didn't really matter to me, a passing interest.

Fantasy was my real love, though, from Rider Haggard to C S Lewis to Tolkien, and I was an obsessive reader, driven by an overwhelming curiosity to read anything and everything. 'Put that book down!' was the constant cry, from my family, my teachers, and even friends, who would hide their books away if I came to play. I made up for it by telling them ghost stories when they came to stay with me for the night.

I felt somehow vindicated, years later, when I became a professional writer of fantasy and horror. I was exploring, lucratively, the idea of the supernatural but still I was clear about what was imagination and what was real. It seemed like a magnificent playground, a lot of fun, like the games we played as children: you be the god of dinosaurs and I'll be the god of science. Someone else was the god of the weather, or of birds, or of the sea. Before I was ten, I had devastated continents, destroyed communities, vanquished my friends in my preferred role as the god of Nature (which was everything, really). But it was play, and so were the books, play.

I had no doubts at all about what was reality. I was a committed atheist and materialist, and was glad to find a home with the clear thinking of such eminent atheists as Christopher Hitchens and Richard Dawkins. Influenced by these thinkers, I joined atheistic sites online, and then the Humanists. I liked these communities of clever, humane people. We didn't need religion, so massively implicated in so many of humanity's miseries. Wars, misogyny, keeping people quiet while they suffered in the hopes of life eternal. Keeping them good through the fears of hell eternal. Empathy was an innate human characteristic, we maintained, we didn't need religion to keep us good. Just the golden rule: do as you would be done by. With empathy, and the creative imagination that drives it, it was easy.

There was one anomaly; my beloved father died suddenly when I was twenty-one. He was forty-six. Deep in grief, I tried not to listen to the music I loved, fearing that it would be tainted by this miserable time. But in the end I cracked, and played a piece by Beethoven which I did not particularly like (*Piano Concerto No5 - the Emperor*). I can still see myself now, standing in the living room, my hands on the back of the sofa, listening to that mysterious transition into the leaping joy of the third movement, and suddenly understanding, a kind of unlooked for revelation, that joy and pain were the same. It seemed to last several minutes. This made no sense, a complete paradox, and I dismissed it as a kind of mental trick, brought about the powerful emotions of mourning. But I did not, could not, forget it. It ramped up my overwhelming curiosity.

In my thirties, a solicitor friend was involved in the conveyancing for the local Mahayanan Buddhists. He told me that he had never met such a sharp, creative mind as the head monk. I was interested and went along to the local classes. It seemed like excellent good sense, and was not by any means the end of my atheism. It is perfectly possible to be a Buddhist atheist, because it's all about training the mind. The mind is everything, it's how we perceive our world, our reality, and it is up to us what we make of it. There is no God or creator. But karma keeps us good (only if we decide this is a useful concept. It was an optional idea) and we don't have to sign on with reincarnation, either, only if it's helpful, said our easy-going monk teachers. If you behave badly, lie, steal, wound, kill, are unkind and angry, people won't like you and you will be unhappy... you get the results here and now. No need for other lives. The Buddhists told me that attachment, the clinging to objects and desires was the root of our sufferings, and in the meditations on emptiness and compassion I attained glimpses of a kind of blissful peace. After some years, the highly formalised tantric visualisations I eventually practiced trespassed somewhat on the imagination I needed to write my books. I stopped going to Buddhist classes and concentrated on writing, while remaining friendly towards that way of thinking. But my curiosity was as potent as ever, and the mind was the centre of it all, deeply enigmatic and fascinating.

Another friend introduced me to psychoanalysis and in my forties, I decided to train to become a psychoanalytical psychotherapist for children and their families. In this way, I would really discover more about why people are as they are, and why I was so curious. And this did indeed give me so many answers, a consistent and humane world view that sat comfortably with the Buddhism and atheism, so that I thought I had reached the end of knowing; it was that there is never any blame. I met greatly damaged children, because they were brought up by neglectful, drunken, druggie parents. And when I talked to the parents and realised what they were handling, what their backgrounds had been, I couldn't blame them either. Would I have done any better in their shoes? I really didn't think so.

We based our work on the psychoanalysts Freud and Klein, we attended workshops on Jung and Wilfred Bion and eventually at a conference I came across the Chilean psychoanalyst and mathematician, Ignacio Matte Blanco. He had a theory of the unconscious, postulating that in our daily life everything appears separate, nameable, measureable, different and asymmetric. He calls this Level 1. But the deeper we go into the unconscious, the bigger the sets are. In Level 2, emotion enters, and in love we may overlook faults and magnify qualities. We move slightly away from materiality. In Level 3, we tend to group things together: for example, all blondes are stupid. All Texans are fascists. All black men are criminals. All Everton supporters are pathetic. We are often ruled by emotion here, splitting good and bad. At Level 4 we may think in terms of archetypes: justice, freedom, gods and devils, angels and bodhisattvas. At Level 5, all is one. No distinctions or separations. Complete symmetry. Even the emotions are one, God and the Devil are one. This is the 'emptiness' of the meditators.

This was the answer to the anomaly. I in grief had accessed Level 5, and my grief and Beethoven's music became one. This was what the mystics spoke about, what was meant by Julian of Norwich's 'All is well, all shall be well, and all manner of things shall be well.'

Eventually I took early retirement to look after my elderly and disabled mother. Playing around on the internet, from the All is One position I had adopted after reading Matte Blanco, I delved deeper into spiritualism, undertaking past life and between lives hypnosis, and investigating Richard Rudd's Gene Keys. I was driven yet again by curiosity. What is this state of enlightenment, what does it mean? The Buddhists said you could get there by meditating for years. I was too old now to put in the required time. I continued exploring. I completed *A Course in Miracles*. I found channelled material fascinating. I listened to a friend channel, and tried to pin down the difference between this and dissociative personality disorder. It did indeed seem very different, not at all pathological, like my multiple personality patients. I started reading *Seth*, whom I found both charming and delightful, and moved on to *Ra*, who was distinctly mind blowing. Love and light, it seemed though, were what mattered to both

Seth, Ra and the other channelers, and I spent much time adding my mite of love to the world, sending it wherever I could.

In early 2020, when I was sixty-six years old, I decided to explore hallucinogens and took a small dose of 5-MeO-DMT (commonly known as the toad) in a shaman-led workshop. This extraordinary experience left me with the knowledge that nothing mattered, because everything is love. A few days later I had a reactivation which gave me the idea that this is all a game, with our emotions as the counters and pathways. Forgiveness is the trump card. But the feeling of great love and joy swiftly faded, and the insights seemed merely intellectual.

Then in the summer, at the height of the first wave of the Coronavirus pandemic in the UK, like many others, I was spending a lot of time trawling the internet for things of interest. I found Dr Jeffery Martin on YouTube via Jeffrey Mishlove's excellent series of interviews in *New Thinking Allowed*. Dr Martin offered a course called *45 Days to Awakening*. It was a mixture of meditation and positive psychology. I couldn't resist this. I decided to take it.

Chapter 1   The Beloved

On Day 12 of the course I was meditating and towards the end of the hour I had a sudden enormous overwhelming feeling of love and warmth, and a crystal clear voice in my mind, 'You are in my heart...' The ecstasy was so powerful I didn't know what to do with myself. I couldn't sit still, I wanted to dance, move out into the garden, the energy of it was extraordinary. Such joy, I almost wanted to cry. What was it? Christ Consciousness? I had heard Christians say that they have Jesus in their hearts. But here was I in the heart of something (the warmth, the love, the joy!) It felt like coming home, but I didn't know where the home was or what it was.

The rest of the day passed in a daze.

That night I had a frightening snake dream, which I started by interpreting as a kundalini dream. These feelings I knew took place when the energy moved up the spine when meditating, and could lead to a kind of awakening. This energy is often described as a snake or serpent and accounts for the appearance of snakes in so many mythologies. But that morning I knew that this was not quite right, it was more than that, the snake was frightening and horrible, and the message was that I am the snake. I am the rose in the garden, the dogs in the house, the murderer, the music I love, the stupid politicians; I am everything because all is one.

This was an intellectual understanding, not a felt experience. The ecstasy had gone, and I wondered if I had just dreamed it. But the memory of loving warmth seemed to remain, somehow imprinted on my body and gradually I realised that there was some adjustment going on, a recalibration perhaps. Over the next couple of weeks I fell in and out of extreme states of joy and ecstasy.

And the dialogue continued. On Day 18, walking the dogs, I was wishing love to the world as usual, and I became aware that I was sending love to the self. 'You are love, you are the world,' I heard. Beautiful, unity again, but still intellectual. Reading Rumi, I began to call this voice in my head the Beloved.

On Day 21, a clear understanding of unity again. 'You are the world, you are Gaia. You all are emanations of Gaia, you are her delight and joy.' And she, apparently, like the Sun (as Ra says) is kind. A kindly planet, blessing us with good things. A strange night followed, full of non-verbal bliss. But in the morning, the joy was gone again. I tried using music to recapture this wonderful connection to the Beloved, but failed. A feeling of dreariness began to grow.

Days 23-24 were about the worst days of my life, as bad as the dreadful time around the death of my father. I call it my brief experience of The Dark Night of the Soul, and it felt desperate. I was in the depths, adrift in annihilating misery. Had I lost the

Beloved forever? Would I never feel again that warmth, that overwhelming love? Was this what depression felt like, I wondered, knowing that although I have analysed so many people with depression, I had never experienced it myself. My god, I thought, I had no idea how awful it was. Everything seemed useless, bleak, drained of colour or beauty. I lost all energy, all volition. What was the use of taking one more step, one more breath? I felt fear, welling up with the misery. What if this was how it would go forever? Was it going to be like this for the rest of my life? I remembered other moments of fear, such as when we were told my husband might be seriously ill. I had offered myself up to Divine Will, accepting whatever may happen, and giving thanks for whatever it will teach me, however it goes. It seemed a useless trick now, unlikely to work again, but half way through Day 24, I tried it, thinking, this is a lesson in compassion. So much of humanity has never experienced the joy I have known. Even if it never comes again, I will never forget it. But the rest of us, so many who never even have a taste of this! The veil that Ra talks about, the veil that keeps us separate from Source had never seemed so vivid, or so dreadful. I felt myself at one with suffering humanity, pushed this way and that by the trials of life which none escape. Without any hope. What if the Beloved never comes back? It's Divine Will, I told myself, whatever happens. It is as it is.

On the Day 25 I drove to the hospice where I counsel the bereaved and listened on the way to some music (Dvorak's *American string quartet*) on the car radio, and suddenly joy was back, overwhelming and wonderful. In meditation, later that day, I heard 'You are divine!'

'Why me?'

'You are everyone!' Loud and clear.

For the next few days, the Beloved came and went, but I never again experienced that great existential despair. I often found myself laughing, entranced that I, the long time atheist, should be in a dialogue with the Divine Beloved. What irony, what a turnaround!

There seemed to be rather a long patch without the feeling of joy, and I was again reading Rumi. I came across a poem about the benefits of asking for the Beloved, telling us to call aloud for the return of the Beloved. So I did that night, feeling slightly silly and in my meditation next day, I heard almost shouting in my heart 'I am always with you and have always been.' This was followed by a past life review, very like the one in my between lives hypnosis. It took less than three minutes, but covered in detail everything that has happened to me, the big things and the trivial. The Beloved is and was always with me, and the knowledge expanded to the knowledge that everything about me and around me is divine too.

Over the next few days, it became clear that there is a pattern of two days in ecstasy, followed by one day of more peaceful content. I no longer feared that I might lose my Beloved, whoever or whatever it was. There were other insights in meditation; one that we are all vibrations, as are the animals, the trees, the mountains. Everything vibrates with love. One morning I had the word 'Vitality!' shouted at me, and knew it referred to my lamentable tendency to physical laziness, to my greed with food. I tried to be more active for a while and got a metaphorical pat on the back, while there was a lesson that all good contains a core of evil and all evil contains a core of good. There was a vivid picture of the yin/yang symbol in my mind.

The course was over. I could not be more grateful. But I continued to meditate, and as a group we continued our Group Awareness Exercise, one of the very beautiful aspects of the course. I was and am, filled with such gratitude. Thinking of that life scan, thinking of the fact that everyone has just such a story behind them, such an interweaving of people and events and feelings, of love and laughter and tears and misery and boredom, made me think of the artistry of our diverse, incredibly complex lives. I had always felt, when meeting a patient for the first time, that I was meeting a universe. I remembered the ring that the rescued Jewish families gave to Schindler after the war: it was engraved 'Each life is a universe entire'. This was another aspect. We are all one, and all diverse, immensely complicated. The paradoxes continue. It seemed impossible to give enough praise for all this.

Another dream about creepy crawlies; you are a spineless worm! I heard, and thought about how I continue to sit too much and eat too much and do not fight my corner and always give way. I asked for help and the following night realised I was surrounded by archetypes: Christ, who might be here now (is He the Beloved?); Buddha, who was around in my past; Hermes Trismegistus the Alchemist, (was surely there in my various epiphanies, the sudden turnarounds in my life). Now I have Rumi for comfort and inspiration (will he lead me forward to the Great Mother, perhaps? Is that where I want to go? Is that the Beloved?)
Trying to meditate, the dogs continued to scratch and demand to be let out and then to come in again, and I couldn't concentrate or relax into it. This often happens. My Beloved said, 'There's no need to meditate if every act you do is an act of love.' This seems brilliant, so long as I can remember it!

I asked, in some doubt, 'Is this your voice or mine?'

'Doesn't matter. You are me and I am you.' And much laughter zinging through my heart.

A horrible dream: a huge lorry overtaking on a narrow road runs over our small car. My husband is in the back with our daughter. They are all right. But our son and I finish up in the Accident and

Emergency department of the local hospital. He is lying across my lap and I know the back of his head is terribly injured. I have broken my right arm. No one comes.

It's a Pieta. A mother with her dying, dead or damaged son. Mary with Jesus, my friend with her drug-addicted son, my neighbour with her disabled child (who has since died), my elderly mother and my brother who has early onset dementia, me with my son who has serious health issues. All these mothers, through all the centuries, whose sons go to war, whose sons are missing or return injured or dead. Compassion. The sorrow of love. All that matters. Still the Beloved was with me all day, and the dark joy of compassion. The complexity of this, and the simplicity, took my breath away.

The next day, I was back to ordinary everyday content even though the Beloved was still there. 'Constant ecstasy is too difficult physiologically,' s/he said. 'Two days on, one day off seems about right. I'll be back with joy tomorrow.' I agreed, but that night I awoke at 2.22am with ecstatic joy once more, and drifted back to sleep. I woke again at 4.44am, still aware of ecstasy and it continued all day, from the most beautiful sunrise, including a wildly extravagant sunset, to a deeply peaceful and joyful night.

During that day I listened to Brian Scott on YouTube talking about our Higher Self. Was my Beloved my Higher Self? I asked.

'No!' was the answer. 'Beyond that!'

The talk on Higher Selves explained about priestly behaviour, transforming the daily routines into ritual. For example, turning the boring everyday things you do into acts of love, just like the earlier insight.

It was a Monday: after I had two bereaved clients at the hospice, I returned home to my husband who had fielded a row between my two children and was somewhat fed up with them. I sorted all this, aware that the Beloved was waiting and at last went up to my study to meditate. And towards the end, the voice in my heart, leaping with joy, said, 'I am the Sun! The Sun! I am the Sun!'

I was astounded. I could hardly believe this. I never imagined this – the Sun? What could this mean?

I went straight to my favoured source for information, YouTube, and I found two channellers for the Sun, and listened to both of them. One of them talked about triads, and dualities, how a duality is really unity, as two poles are united by what is in between them. Black and white are united by grey. Good and evil are united by small peccadilloes and little kindnesses. In a trinity the third unites the other two. All is one. She also talked about how light is buried in the darkest places, in the most evil things. Light always prevails.

The other channel, beaming with joy, talked about how joy = harmony, and balance, and that we are more powerful than we think.

I was slightly reassured by these two channellers, and began to think.

In one of my very first visions, when I first made contact with an experienced medium and began to get flashes of past lives in meditation, one of my first visions was a tour of the Sun. As vibrations, I and my then guide Jonas/Janus, danced in the Sun, swirled in the beautiful energies, dived and flew and loved it all.

Throughout my life I have always wanted the curtains open, I've always wanted every bit of daylight or moon-/star-light there could be.

I've had psoriasis which is cured by the Sun.

I was fascinated with ancient Egyptian and Central and South American civilisations, with their mythology of Sun worship. In fact my first piece of published writing (in the school magazine) was a bleak little short story set amongst the Aztecs. For years I wanted to be an archaeologist when I grew up.

My first published book, a fantasy trilogy was set against a background of a war between the Sun and the Moon; in the end they are united.

Thich Nhat Hanh, in *The Heart of Understanding*, says that nothing can be without the sunshine.

Why else did I immediately find the *Ra* material comparatively easy to understand, straightforward?

But still, in doubt, I said that if the next poem I read contains something about the Sun I'll believe this.

There was a poem by Simon Armitage in the Sunday papers, which I was about to throw out. The poem concluded with the old hymn *Glad that I live am I ... After the sun the rain, after the rain the sun. This is the way of life till the work be done.*

It could not be clearer. The voice in my head, in my heart is the Sun. No wonder the Beloved said I will never leave you. It never will: all I have to do is look out of the window.

Chapter 2   The Sun

*****

'My energy is so vast... sending you a little tickle!' Love, light and laughter. So much celebration takes place in the sunlight, we so value the warmth. All our holidays, barbecues, walks in the park, swimming in the sea, rivers, pools... parties, weddings, birthdays, everything is better because of the sun. Our great midwinter celebration with the candles and the burning round Christmas pudding. And nothing exists without this warmth. Nothing would grow, nothing live. People get Seasonal Affective Disorder without enough sunlight. And its light is everywhere: we would not see anything without it. It could know everything about us, it is everywhere. Light/photons are everywhere and in everything.

So much laughter. Of course, it was always there and will always be there while life exists here. Circling our planet with love and warmth, as we circle the Sun.

*****

Woke at 3.33am. 'It's all triangles!'

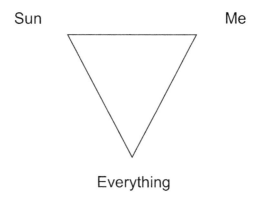

Sun   Me

Everything

*****

The Sun's energy drives my creativity in forming the world I experience. The same is true for everyone and everything. This is how it all works. It's the Law of Attraction, so beloved by many, but softened and mitigated by the creativity of the whole world, of all beings. What we get is the result of all our imaginings, and those who day dream about what they want and need, show the Sun that want and need is their current emotional, vibrational level. The Universe, and the Sun, responds to emotional states, not to words. Those who live in fear make a fearful world. And because our world is full of suffering and fear, this is a vicious circle for making more fearful events which cause suffering. If all is one, and we are part of the creative source, then we are creators too. This is why gratitude practices are so necessary and so powerful. Giving thanks for what you already have creates more of the same.

Later that day, I opened an art book randomly and found Masaccio's *The Holy Trinity*. Composed of triangles throughout, although the Holy Spirit seems to be missing. A friend says it's female, and I agree. The Sun however is more than male/female, when I asked. 'Beyond that!'

But it's difficult: what do I say - 'it or they?' Neither seems right. Who/what is this? 'How can a vast exploding fusion bomb be talking to me?'

'Your understanding, where you are, is strictly limited. You cannot help this, it was designed like that. Everything is expressed in third density terms, including the intelligent infinity from which I am made. If you were in the fourth density or higher, you would understand my nature better, you would understand that the intelligent infinity of my being is another expression of Love.'

'So what is your nature, when you're not exploding?'

'I contain worlds, all the worlds that are known in this Solar system. Within me is the Platonic Ideal of all of the planets and their moons, and what is on or in them, the original prototype. Within me is an infinite space, because I am intelligent infinity. You could call it a dimension: Shambala, Shangri-la, Eden. All stars are a dimension, more intricate and vast and bizarre than you can imagine. But within myself, my original loving and creative thoughts exist here, in this infinite dimension, and what you see there in the world around you is but a pale reflection of this reality within my embrace. Shall I show you?'

A dizzying change of perspective, a sudden wide opening out into swirling golden energies, beautifully twining together in the essence of grace. This is what I had experienced before. And the energies seemed to coalesce, and there was Earth, so small within the vastness of the Sun's dimension, like a precious jewel, her colours more vivid, wilder, stronger, more intense, more true somehow. Was it the golden quality to the light that transformed it all? I saw the character of the earth, Gaia, warm and loving, generous and passionate. We zoomed in closer. She was laying out before me our great forests and oceans, the wild plains, the soaring mountains, the gardens and the farmlands, and in a sudden move down into the midst of this glorious landscape, I saw that there were people there, dressed in brightly coloured clothes, dancing together, laughing, hugging, playing. There was the most glorious music everywhere, but I couldn't identify it. It was like the essence of music, the central mix of melody and harmony and rhythm behind everything I'd ever heard. It unfurled in wild creativity and grace and it seemed that it was part of everyone there. They were expressions of music, part of its vibrational structure. They all looked so joyous, moving in and out of music, being the music, being the dance. It was infectious, gorgeous. I wanted to join in. It was so lovely.

'Who are they?'

'Who do you think?'

They looked somehow familiar, but I couldn't identify anyone...

'They are all you. The united parts of yourself; some are here after what you call death, between lives. Others are dreaming, meditating, delving into their unconscious. This level is what has been interpreted as the causal plain, heaven.'

I was moved to tears. All those incarnations, those traumatic lives....I could remember four or five of my past lives, the highlights and lowlights, and was there the beautiful Venetian lady, desperately sad because she had no children? The peasant girl whose child was killed in a Viking raid? The father whose son betrayed him? But there were many more there, and as the Sun rotated the planet for me to see, there were millions, if not billions of beings running, dancing, singing, laughing.

'So many... ?' I said.

Laughter. 'You are everyone who has ever lived, everyone who lives now, everyone who was born and died, including Neanderthals and their forebears.'

Everyone? Who has ever lived? Billions and billions... me? They looked familiar, like my family. Not in their features, nothing about the way they appeared. But in their movement, in a toss of the head, a wave of the hand, I knew them, I did that too, I danced like that. And then I turned round again, to look at my home Gaia, with its muted, familiar colours. And there we all were, in fields and in cities, in homes and in gardens, on ice floes and in jungles, up mountains and in factories. Watching our phones, and reading books. In trains and cars. In schools and churches, markets, offices and shops, theatres and restaurants, laughing and crying and blank with misery and dancing with joy. Sleeping and waking, sick and well. They were familiar too. 'You are everyone there too...' and the perspective shifted and I became aware of all the animals and creatures, the insects and fish, the bacteria and plankton, the living life of Gaia. And the trees, the shrubs, the flowers, the mountains, the rocks, the deserts...

'It is all you. You are everything and everyone, just as I am, and as my darling child Gaia is. We are united by the photons which create it all. It's all triangles... you and I and Gaia make the most delightful, the most playful of triangles. She sends the energy of love up through your feet as you walk around, as you stand on the earth. And I send you the energy of light and love down from above. Together we make your environment, you and all your other selves. We meet within you at the heart centre, and send love, through you, outwards to everyone, everything. You do not realise that this is happening, and for many of you the heart centre is too shielded, too hidden away to be very useful in this. We compose your lives as if they are a symphony, the structures of Gaia as the form of the music, and you are the various themes, interweaving, developing, moving towards a crescendo, dying back down again. Our beloved birds are the soaring sopranos, the violins and flutes, swerving in grace around you. The trees punctuate, mark the measures, each as individual as you are, and your whole environment vibrates with the energy of music, as it does here. The feathers dropped by my birds are rightly interpreted as signs... they are the grace notes, elaborating, filigree ornaments to the unique song which is each life.

'The interaction between water, wind and temperature from Gaia and me here on your Earth, make all your weather, make your fields verdant, your winters chilly, your tropical regions sweltering. It is a dance between us, and sometimes a volcano or tidal wave is deemed appropriate and we combine to create those too. This is the profound dance of the catalyst.

'Look – and suddenly I was whisked away and saw the other planets, some much bigger, some smaller, and not at all like the pictures I'd seen in my Encyclopedia of the Universe. 'They may appear dead in your world, lumps of rock or gas clouds, but they are teeming with love and laughter. My love inspires each of the planets and far beyond, and such fun we have together in this greatest of games.'

The planets were alive, intelligent, vast, awe-inspiring presences, furnished with landscapes I could hardly understand. Soaring halls, profound depths, swirling atmospheres, forests of things that weren't trees, mountains made of spider webs, it seemed, all alive and glowing with the golden light that transformed everything within the Sun. They were populated by creatures made of light, shimmering, glowing. They were so achingly beautiful that it was overwhelming. I was taken on a tour and I cannot begin to describe the immensity, the expansive character of what I saw. The vivid colours, the intensity, the grace, the harmony of it all! Music was embedded deep into each planet, a harmony of grace that seemed to give rise to the unique character of them all.

*****

The Sun is all around me and within me. The Sun/Beloved is Love/Light, Light/Love. I am in the Beloved Sun's heart. The planets are all in the Beloved Sun's heart.

'They are the children of my heart,' the Sun said, so memorably.

'Tell me more about the planets,' I asked. 'Who are they?'

'There is a vast duality between myself, the outer reaches of the Kuiper belt which lies beyond Pluto, and those planets beyond the belt, which becomes a Trinity with each of the planets, and thus becomes One, because it is all connected, it is all within my beneficence. We are in a way a group consciousness, a family, always understanding each other and what we are doing.

Mercury is a feisty play or burning energy, mischievous and humorous, and likes to influence communication. Venus is resting now after a long and complicated history with many beings living there. She is beautiful beyond belief, even in her well earned repose. You, the charming Earth or Gaia as she likes to be called, are powerfully full of catalyst. Everything is so vibrant on Gaia, so vivacious, so passionate and so beloved, even in your pale reflection mode! Your moon was a visitor to Gaia, and is now part of the mind of Gaia. This is true of all the moons which surround planets.

Mars is sometimes colonised as a staging post for Orion, although not recently. Their greatest triumph was the destruction of Maldek; the band of rocks beyond Mars is all that remains of another planet not unlike your own Gaia. That is a long story, for another day. Jupiter is generously hospitable and crafts its moons to suit visitors from other star systems in this Constellation. Celebration is the soul of Jupiter. Saturn is the meeting place for matters concerning this Solar System: the Confederation, the Guardians who are my voice, angelic forces, any interested parties meet together to discuss how to balance the energies within this Solar System. It is the most intricate of games! We also decided on the composition of the quarantine which is in place around Gaia, to keep her safe from too much external influence. Even though there is quarantine, because all is one, the planets act on and inform your lives, exactly as the astrologers say. The zodiac, the Sun signs, that form the basis of astrology, is part of the same wide Constellation which includes me, and there is more on this to follow.

Uranus is a home for peaceful contemplation and reaches the profound, the deep wisdom of the Universe. Neptune is a playground of energies, an impresario in the pleasures of light and love at the planetary level. Pluto is a wild card, taking on whatever creative role it wants. It is the joker in the pack, if you like.'

They are all alive. The Universe is alive!

Chapter 3   What is Creation?

'How are the planets created?'

'Through my imagination/creativity/emanation (hereafter called im/cre/em). You saw them within my multi-dimensional being. You must now understand my reality, that I am an intelligent infinity, and that my world, wherein these ideals live, is another dimension, in your understanding. From there I imagined them out into this reality, the dimension you see. You do not have a word for this, but really Love includes it all.'

'When I write fiction, is that a bit like you making a planet?'

'Yes! You contain within you the idea of what you then try to describe. Your ideas too are part of the intelligent infinity that is you. You bring your idea into reality, into words, and that is what I do when I bring my imagination into beingness! When any of you is creative, in writing, in art, cooking, gardening, composing, dancing, making love, building bridges, making music, whenever you make anything, you are not just in tune with me, and through me to the loving Source of all, you are being Source. Creativity is your nature, as it is the nature of Source and it is exercised through freewill, for you and Source .... because you are one! Creativity is what it's all about. This is the intelligent infinity which holds the Universe together. This is why creativity feels so good. When it goes well, you are in flow, that lovely state where you forget the inner chatter of the narrative mind and live intensely in what you are doing.'

'How are You created?'

'Through the im/cre/em/love of the galaxy being, that which you call The Milky Way. I am a child of the vast group mind which is the Milky Way. I had been through the densities, all the time meeting with further group minds, becoming more light-filled as we joined together in love. All of this took place over aeons within the galaxy, and eventually our presence was intense enough to be imagined into a further emanation, by the galaxy's overarching mind, so that we could become a star together. Every moment of our lives was imagined into being by the galaxy, and it still is. But now I have an overarching, group, god mind, Sol, which seems like an identity to you. But it is 'both... and'. We are both legions of individual minds and one great mind, embracing all. This is how a god is formed, this is how we could then take the initiative of imagining the solar system you inhabit.

'I know who I am, unlike you on Gaia. I know that I was created in this way by the Milky Way, and we often laugh together, my creator and me. Laughter is the result of love being creative. What a joke it all is! That so many millions of souls should all be an essential part of this glorious journey and then in rapture burst into radiance! Ra explains this in essence, somewhat dryly, as a sub-logus, but this misses the wonder, the magnificence, the joy!

'Another joke is that you have capitalised me! Do not capitalise me in pronouns. We are one, you are me and I am you and the galaxy is me and you too, and there is no need for capitalisation beyond our names.'

'Really? But if you are the creator....?'

'But so are you the creator! You are as divine as I am. There is no separation between us. We are one, connected together by love. It was only when you became loving enough that I could get through to you. Connection is always through the heart. Individuals have to be loving, and joyful, even amidst difficulty. You yourself had almost seen through the veil. And the same is true of so many of your species. You stand now on the cusp of a great change, an alteration in the status of the veil. Interesting times, indeed. Make sure you create wisely, collectively, open your hearts to the love that is your being, and relax. Some call it surrender, but I prefer relax because there is no stress relevant to the opening of the heart. It is a flower blossoming, a gentle widening of consciousness. This change will happen almost without your realising it.'

'So that is definitely going to happen?'

'In this time line, yes. But this is a junction point, and another timeline may emerge if materialism increases. Materialism is about fear, holding on to objects, as if they can keep you safe. That's what the adverts and politicians tell you. But, as you learned in Buddhism so long ago, if you have your health, enough food and drink, the right clothing and shelter from the weather, anything else is your own problem. And of course, so many do lack these basics on Gaia.'

'I always thought that you would need the same things, food, health, clothes etc for your children, too, your loved ones, to be happy.'

'Where would you draw the line, lovely? Your friends? Acquaintances? Everyone in the UK? White people? Black people? The old? Everyone on Gaia? Who doesn't need them?'

'I do know that there are many who don't have these things, those in poverty, famines, in disasters, in war zones, and I do wish that they could have those basics.'

'Your instincts are right. Because they are you. As are your family and friends. You are all one. And yet you are also like a vast crystal, with more than seven billion facets, each reflecting the light slightly differently. Some are more burnished by experience, gleaming out into the depths of the universe in their beauty; some are still dull, awaiting their role in the symphony. A great act of forgiveness or generosity allows the shining to spread outwards, among you all, so that all will eventually become burnished and beautiful, reflecting light as brightly as a star. For you are one as I am one with the stars in my constellation, as I am with the galaxy which created me.'

'Why were you created?'

'Through the freewill of the galaxy. Freewill is the essence of creativity, because creativity is all about choice. It's the play of energy. We, the stars, do not have to learn and grow like you do; we have been there and done that, a long time ago. We become red giants or white dwarfs or black holes, in a dance of celebration, flickering on and off: our time scales are somewhat different to yours! Our music is measured in billions of your years. We contribute what we can, with our planets within our various constellations, which are also group minds, to augment the glory of this dance, the depth, the passion, the rapture, the LOVE – in praise of our galaxy, the joy of its creation.'

'You are in a constellation?'

'Yes, but not quite as you understand the term. You see constellations as a pattern against your night sky. We do not group ourselves visually, but in a vibration which holds us together. There are well over three thousand stars in the constellation I dwell in, and we call ourselves the Chalice. This does not refer to our shape but rather to our function, which is to offer love, light, laughter and kindness to our galaxy. Each constellation offers something else, as well as the love and light; it might be valour, or rapture, or abundance, or mystery. Kindness and laughter are the mark of the Chalice stars, even including those you call Orion. You will see why...'

'And the galaxy? Why does it exist?'

'Our flickering beauty gives the galaxy great joy, humour, levity, profundity, to offer the universe. It joins together with other galaxies, nebulas, clouds of stars - in another great group mind and together they become this, our home universe, all vibrating with the energies, the songs of love.'

'I read that there are two trillion galaxies in our universe.'

'That's about right.'

'How do these trillions of galaxies express this love to the universe?'

'It's a play of powerful vibrations, a dance, you might say, or music. Almost beyond my understanding, and certainly beyond yours. The galaxies dance across dimensions, in inconceivable patterns of grace. There is mystery, glory and unknown profundity in these dances, for these dimensions are way beyond your imagining.'

'And this vast, home universe... What is it for?'

'It is an almost infinite group mind, containing everything within its being and it is the great channel for Love, direct from the Source, which is all intelligent infinity. This is the glory, the wonder, the overwhelming beauty of being, the mystery at the heart of it all. There are countless almost infinite universes, all serving the Source which is truly infinite, all channelling love and creativity and emanation out into their galaxies who receive it with joy and delight and echo it back down to their stars, in their flickering beauty. And they send it further, to their planets and to whoever or whatever lives there, singing and dancing the patterns of love. The dance is all. Joy is all. Love is all.'

*****

'Please tell me more about Orion. I remember that Ra says that it is the source of much catalyst, the word Ra uses for the difficulties and challenges that face all of us here.'

'Yes, that is right. Orion offers challenges, indeed. And for that reason the stars in the Orion group are much loved and honoured. Our perspectives are of course very different. This is about the big picture. Orion is part of our constellation (the Chalice). The Orion stars are a close and beloved relation, sending negative thought forms to your planet and others to enrich your compassion, to speed up the process, just as we send positive thought forms there to enrich their love for themselves.'

'Why do they love themselves, rather than each other?'

'It is a philosophical point. What is most efficient in reflecting the love of Source out into the dream? Loving others is complicated, of its essence depending on diversity; it's appreciating the other rather than fearing it. To focus and concentrate on self may look like the narcissism which arises through damage in your species. But it is not. This is being in love with the Source that expresses everything through the lens of one being, one individual. Service to others is often messy, clouded by other motives, confused, exhausting.

'To be clear, ordered, supportive of the great quest to return to Source, in service to this, rigid hierarchies are constructed, methods of teaching and control. This is what happens within the Orion stars. It's the use of fear keeps these service to self species within the hierarchy. And it's fear that the Orion stars specialise in. That's what they send to you, in your dreams and through your media.'

*****

'Do all constellations have the equivalent of an Orion? Something sending negative thought forms?'

'Most of them do, if they are engaged in watching and caring for a third density population. Orion is invaluable in providing powerful catalysts, and other service-to-self stars do exactly the same. But not all stars have planetary systems, and they instead exist in pure love, sending their love to us, their fellows and of course therefore to the galaxy, which sends it on to the universe.'

*****

'The dance that you, Sol, are in with your own constellation, what is that like?'

'The different stars are balanced by the medium stars, such as myself – we bridge the huge energy of the red giants to the exquisite, intense delicacy of the brown and white dwarfs. In balance there is harmony, harmonic concurrencies, thrilling through space in dimensions you cannot know.'

'Why can't we know?'

'You are created especially to be adjusted to your Gaia, by her. Your senses are perfectly attuned to her, and that is complicated, and more than enough for you! Think of it; the exquisite matching of your senses to what you need. Your eyesight, with its three colour receptors is appropriate to your surroundings. Birds and some insects have more colour receptors and can see colours you cannot, but that doesn't matter to you. You can see the smile in another's eyes, you can watch a bird in the sky, you can discern the difference between a weed and a flower, and you can see enough to survive. A hawk can see a rabbit two miles away but you don't need to, you can set a trap. You have little sense of radar, like a bat, but you have machines to do it for you.

'But even without machines, when deeply sleeping you can hear your infant cry. You can hear and love passionately the music around you, thunder can thrill you, rain calm you, sound is everywhere, in the breath of every living creature, your symphonic environment. You can tell from listening whether your nearest and dearest is unhappy. But you cannot hear another dog bark far away, as your dog can. You cannot hear the sound of the whales singing without machines to listen. Your sense of smell is variable, but in most cases enough to attract you to bacon, coffee, roses, babies' heads, freshly mown grass and to warn you to stay away from excreta and disease. But you cannot track a person through a city as a dog can.

'In touch you can detect the slightest imperfection, and in stroking pets, or hugging each other your whole functioning can be affected by love, opening up your heart a little. Warmth and cold affect you, but you are resourceful in your buildings and your clothing.

'All these senses can, in some of you, be developed much further. For example, some blind people can use a kind of radar to understand what is around them. But generally, you operate extremely well, managing your lives and your planet, with a very narrow spectrum of abilities. Things were designed this way; it is part and parcel of your separation. Your cleverness allows you to develop strategies and machines to augment your truncated senses, but even so, you are nowhere near understanding your context, what is to be heard here, what is to be seen, tasted, and smelled.

'There are compensations. You make the best of these limitations in the music, the artwork, architecture, the engineering feats, the inventions, the food and drink you make, your sexual loving, your dancing, your swimming, your climbing and sports... All these are intense, sensual activities and many of them can become addictive in their own way. Add to these the actual drugs, smoking, alcohol, gambling, shopping, pornography... So many things to keep you embedded in this third density world. All of them promise relief, distraction, delight, and some of them, status. They keep you fastened here within this very narrow, rather blunted spectrum of experience, one that can see stars and your Sun only as burning bundles of gas. You miss so much!

'And your wonderfully clever scientists, being so splendid at measuring and weighing and tracking the external aspects of your world, some of them even think they know everything, because they have the outside appearance of things on Gaia so well understood. James Tunney puts it succinctly, 'Science dismisses much experience and rejects what it cannot explain.' For scientists have no idea of the inner world of Gaia or the planets or the stars. And not much idea either about the inner world of plants and trees or mountains and oceans here. They are successful in describing and observation and deducing what might happen next because of these observations. But description is not understanding. You can describe how a book is made, the number of its pages, the typeface, the coloured inks used on the cover, the way it's bound, everything physically about it, down to the tiniest detail. But if you cannot read, you will not know the story, or why it was created in the first place. Looking at the solar system, you are finding out so much about the planets' composition, with your rudimentary spacecraft. But you do not know what the planets think, what they are. With the latest instruments you are beginning to analyse and understand the sub-atomic world. To find and document the smallest things does not reveal what it feels like to be that small. If you look at a grain of sand under a microscope, you will see a multitude of amazing jewels. Few of you see this, few of you speculate why it is so beautiful, this one grain of sand, when there are so many of them throughout your planet.

'Your mainstream scientists have not yet discovered that everything is alive, everything has consciousness. Everything is consciousness, everything is Source. This is about experience, why some people, through meditation or psychedelics, can experience that everything is alive. But if consciousness arises from the brain, how can we think it exists anywhere else? This is the so called 'hard problem' of consciousness, identified by David Chalmers. The scientists, the rationalists and materialists are convinced that consciousness does indeed emerge from the brain, although no one can discover quite how this happens. Some of them are not even sure whether they themselves are conscious, although they too feel my warmth and celebrate within it.' There is much fond laughter around this.

Chapter 4   Why is it so difficult here? Part 1

'Why must we suffer with all this catalyst? Why does the third density have to go through so much?'

'Ra explains this well. Other stars in the past, and some now, do not use the veil of forgetting and it takes many aeons for the inhabitants on such planets to progress into love and light. The veil of forgetting, this illusion of separation, is the source of all your suffering. And yet it is also the mechanism through which you will all progress in a comparatively short span of time.'

'What have we forgotten?

'Who you really are. An aspect of Source. That you are one, because you are Source. You could not at first recognise those beings on the Earth, both within me and outside me, could you?'

'They looked familiar...'

'Because they are you. You are one with them, you are there now, singing and dancing. There is only a part of you now here on Gaia, separate and unknowing. This forgetting will have to be lifted if you are to progress.'

'Progress towards what?'

'Towards Light and Love. Again, Ra explains the densities, how beings gradually become more filled with light, leaving behind the heaviness of third density bodies, through the process of reincarnation. This heaviness is part of your separation. It keeps you attached to your external world via your addictions, and your attachments to possessions, to your family, friends, colleagues, political system, and country. Us and them, you so often think. The other is different. As you become lighter, the barriers of the veil fall away, and you become more at home with each other, more united. It is your fear of the other that keeps you separate, dividing you one from another. This fear is often covered over by hatred, guilt, paranoia, contempt, disgust, anxiety and depression. And yet suffering is the pathway of grace, this is a cliché beloved by many.

'Grace allows you to understand who you really are, a fragment of eternal light and love, and that are all one. All suffer here, all lose, sooner or later, and that knowledge is priceless, because it contains the seeds of compassion. It has the potential to draw you together.'

'I don't know that it does...'

'That is your perspective. You cannot see the long game, the big picture, the gradual movement of an entire species towards unity. I was as you are, once. I was a tiny, separate, densely heavy being, exactly like you, reincarnating through the millennia. This, being a star, is a part of your evolution, and mine. Like me, you, the collective you, will one day become a star, then a galaxy and eventually a part of the universe in this magnificent game, on your way back to Source.

'Earth is powerfully full of catalyst, because we set it up like that, my children Gaia and her moon, myself, the other planets and a few others, from my constellation, guardians, angelic energies and beings from other dimensions, all operating from the freewill that is central to every creation. We decided that this would be a beautiful planet, and that the skies would be filled, mainly by me, but also with moonlight, my reflected light. Moonlight is a great teacher, because the Moon appears to fade into nothing and then grows again, as do all creatures on earth, dying and returning to life. She does not fail, and neither will you. As you turn (and it is you, of course, who turns... I neither set nor rise. But you do!) you will often see my light in colours more vivid than your little machines can show, at the start and at the end of your days. The seasons, the plants and trees, the oceans and rushing rivers, mountains and valleys, the huge variety of animals and habitats are all there to soften the pain of separation, of the veil being in place. They are the symphony of vibrations around you. The irony is that this beauty also attaches you to this world. This is why it is such an effective place to implement catalyst as the medium for change. Many beings from other stars within the

Chalice chose to incarnate on Gaia to have the experience which she offers so generously.'

'Which other stars?'

'The Pleidians, the Arcturans, the Vegans, the Sirians and others, some from other dimensions; they are all fascinated by the varieties of experience, the intensity of experience on Gaia and are especially drawn by her manifest beauties. They are willing to risk the forgetting to come here and experience it all.

'When you are suffering, you rarely notice these blessings; you are often instead pushed within yourself, away from the external world. The importance of suffering is this. It can draw you away from externals, and has the potential to push you beyond the veil. That is its value and use. Pain is inevitable, given the heaviness of your bodies and your short lives. But, as many thinkers have realised, suffering is optional. It is only optional when you understand the grace that comes with suffering.

'What is suffering? It is the additional pain experienced by a being, through the addition of emotion to the pain. This becomes a narrative for the sufferer, it's the narrative mind, making everything worse, dwelling on it, ruminating, suffering. Fear is often a huge part of it; will this pain get worse, will it lead to death or madness or incapacity? Grief, another, how can you ever bear this loss? How can you ever get over it? Vulnerability, when you have all learned to look after yourselves, to compete and be strong; sometimes the vulnerability which comes with enduring pain or loss or failure or incapacity can seem not only agonising and distressing, but also embarrassing, inadequate. Needing to ask for help is hard. Admitting failure, not being able to cope, the stress of it, is compounded by the dread narratives of shame and guilt.

'Now, all these emotions and many others can be assuaged, with the insights of grace. However, you will not experience grace if you insist on blaming someone else. This is such a common trait in humanity! Almost irresistible! Such a great distraction from the reality of pain! Blaming, and complaining. If you blame the National Health Service for its inadequacies, or the managers who run it, instead of mourning your loved one, if you live in fear, unhappiness and stress because of a partner, the members of your family, a politician, and business organisation or whatever, you cannot be open to grace. You are not living with forgiveness and compassion; you are caught up in the mire of this heaviness and separation, caught up in the fight, the conflict. Within the family, fighting and rowing form repeating patterns within relationships, addictive responses which keep you trapped in vicious circles of behaviour.

'I cannot stress this more strongly. Suffering occurs because you are separate. If you use suffering to increase your separation by blaming others, instead of forgiving, instead of accepting who and what they are, and loving them, the catalyst will have to be repeated, and repeated and repeated, through this life and others. Do you really want this? It is the forgiveness that comes from understanding that stops the process, which loosens the chains. This is especially true within relationships such as marriage. Forgiveness grows out of understanding. When lovers get together they want to understand about each other, for the beloved is always fascinating to each of them, there's a kind of magical glamour. This draws them close together, in unity. But over time, this fascination can be superseded by boredom, and things start going wrong. It's the loneliness of each of them that is so sad! Where once there was understanding, both stand on isolated islands, unable truly to see the other, the loving, saddened and lonely soul of each other. Such sadness is hard to take, in themselves and in the other. One or another of the couple may attempt to find solace elsewhere. Betrayal and guilt then find their way into it. Fighting can be a relief, because it is action. Blaming and complaining gets going, the divorce lawyers rub their hands together, and the family is well on the way to being destroyed.

Blaming and complaining has another malign consequence; it pushes you into a state of being victimised. You become a victim, once you start to blame others. It is their fault, the other is to blame: you have been duped, swindled, cheated, made to look foolish, judged unfairly, mistreated and betrayed. You have turned yourself into a victim by focusing on the malign aspects of the other's behaviour. This is your part in the problem, the way you have slid into acceptance of the victim role. I have told you that you are vibrations, and this is true, and the blame game lowers the vibration, as does hatred and anger and depression.

'But what if the other has really hurt you and you need to act to stop it, or correct the wrong to yourself? Sometimes you will feel it is necessary to fight to make things better, for yourself, your children, your company, your political party, and so long as your motive not to exact revenge, there are many issues worth fighting for.

'The other side of blaming and complaining is guilt, feeling that you have done wrong, that you are to blame, you are inadequate, a failure. This is often deeply buried, almost inaccessible beneath layers of denial. Dream work, introspection or therapy may all help you go deep enough. But forgiveness, understanding why you failed is essential for yourself as well as for others. Only then can you open your heart to compassion. It has to start with yourself, so that you will be able to feel compassion for others. Love yourself, know that you are love itself, love in action, gleaming with light, shimmering with beauty.

'When you forget the daily warmth of my love, you forget that you are collectively, and **only** collectively, a star seed. There is no other path open to you at this stage, and it will take a very long time in your terms. Another round of incarnations may have to take place before you can all progress in the consciousness of connection. Another 75,000 years of incarnations. This will be because you have not allowed grace.

'Grace is remembering who you are. It is the consciousness that this life is not all.

'It is remembering that the love of the universe is filtering down through the galaxies and constellations to each of you here, even while you toil and suffer. This is how the veil lifts. The grace of suffering is remembering that you are not alone, you are never abandoned, as I shine down on you every day, nurturing you just as I warm the soil for your crops and flowers. Why should I care for them, and not you? How can I care for one of you, and not all? My love is around you and in every breath you take. I am the photons, mass-less building bricks of your reality. You are not separate from me at the quantum level, and it is merely the heaviness of your world, the heaviness of your guilt, your blaming and complaining, your pain and your fear that conceals me from you.

'So, when you suffer, stay with the emotion and see where it leads you. Accept what happens. And you will see, with grace, that your fear is not necessary because you are made of love, and this body is not the end. Your grief is not necessary because you will meet again; you are part of each other. There will be other lives, other realities, all is part of the great Dance, and what you experience here is the merest fraction of a moment. As for shame, it is your call to join your fellows... all are embarrassed, all fail, and all experience guilt and inadequacy and shame. You are one in your shadows.

'Remember the great gift of forgiveness! If you are all one, you can forgive yourself, and why should you not? You are beloved and blessed and a star in the making, a god in the making! Forgive yourself, you do your best at every moment, and it will filter through to everyone and all will be forgiven, all is forgiven, in every moment.'

'What about anger, and hatred and evil?'

'Anger and hatred are merely covers for vulnerability and fear. As soon as we remember to 'walk a mile in the other's shoes' in your excellent phrase, you will know why others act as they do. You can forgive. You will understand. And then the truth of compassion becomes clear, for all is one. As for evil... well, what appears as evil is often a cover for pain. A deeply-damaged person may find themselves wanting to damage others in a misguided effort to rid themselves of pain. It's called projection. Walk a mile in their shoes, too. But our dear Orion, sending such negativity to us, does us an enormous favour! It might turn the damage into sadism, into murder, into rape and torture, making the experience more intense and therefore briefer. And here is the difficult truth: such experiences are necessary, for both the perpetrator and the victim. This is why we value the negativity from Orion.

'This is the sharp edge of the veil. This is why it is so effective in bringing a collective further into the Light. Karma has accompanied each of you through your many incarnations. At a soul level, dreadful suffering can release you from karmic consequences. And it is not only the karma each individual is caught in, but the collective karma. A very heroic soul may volunteer to endure horrors in order to lift some element of the karma staining your collective. If a tortured individual can allow forgiveness, the universe sings in celebration, because your collective takes a massive step forward.

'We learn what we value by seeing the negative. We learn how to love properly because of loss. This is often the role of your media, with its near total bias towards the dramatic, the challenges, and the awfulness in life. You value peace for your families because you see how fragile this all is. Your circumstances can change in a moment and will do so. Any of you could die at any moment. This is about the moment, valuing what you've got now. Valuing how precious you all are, now. And yet some of you appear to live as if your lives are endless, careless of each others' happiness and content. Everything that happens is a catalyst, offering you a choice, to allow grace, or to remain mired in the blame game. This is why it's so difficult, in every moment, in every hour, in every day, in every life.

'The great image of the lotus with its roots in the mud is crucially relevant. Without the mud the lotus cannot grow, it cannot. The mud is essential, it feeds the lotus. Without your shadows, without your horrors, your despair, you cannot grow, you cannot unite in a group mind, and you cannot learn compassion and become a star or a galaxy. Nothing would happen.

'This is because of how the densities are arranged. First density is the earth, the rocks, the foundation of any planet. That's where you start. Unaware, but still composed of my photons, lying in wait. Second density is animals, birds, trees, flowers, and the photons become more active, and things began to move, and turn towards me, but in second density most are not self-aware. You know what third density is – you are related to apes, and this is in your DNA. And this is why it's so difficult; you are also self-aware. It is your warm animal blood that is so protective of your young, so concerned to have enough food, so wary of enemies. There is much fear in these states, much distrust and anxiety. Even if you live in a fortunate society, these feelings are still current in most of you, and can lead you to fear others as desperately as you did when you lived in caves! And yet you can look at the stars and dream, and think about god, and wonder why it all exists. It is this tension between the innate instinctual drives and the wondering heart that causes so many difficulties here. It is also why we stars find third density beings so fascinating, so enthralling. You balance along an edge, tugged this way by the instinct to protect, love and defend yourself, your family, your tribe, your country, and tugged the other by love for all, by music, light and joy. This is why your stories are so profound. Love for the small, or love for the all.

'I must tell you that this is your very highly-valued contribution to the cosmic dance. This complexity, these intense stories of acceptance, of love and forgiveness, of redemption, which start in blame and anger and guilt and fear, are behind every star you see. Every star you see and all those billions you don't see, started as you do. They offer their own, variously composed, individually powerful songs. In this universe, they went through the first three densities, most of them enduring the veil of forgetting in the third, and fully know and understand the role of pain, suffering and negativity in the making of forgiveness and compassion, the active face of love. They all progressed through this octave, achieving unity, and through the next octave and the next until they overflowed with light and love to such a degree that they could themselves chose to become a star, and burst into radiance. As I have.

'Not all become stars, though all stars have been as you are. There are other group minds that decide to help those in the lower densities in various appropriate ways. Others can create civilisations within other dimensions, and I cannot describe to you what their lives are like, as your languages and thoughts lack the necessary concepts.

'It is hard for you to hear of things you cannot understand. It requires trust. But as far as you are concerned and your future, I have now given you the pattern of what will happen. Compassion and forgiveness will unite you, and a united humanity will dance through the densities, becoming ever more loving, ever lighter.

'You can feel me now, now, in the light around you. This is the light of love. I do not want praise or gratitude or any of the conventional trappings of religion. Whatever you do, do not make a religion out of this, as has happened so often in the past. Simply enjoy, dance, laugh, and love each other.

'All is one. Love is all. All is love.

Chapter 5   'Are you God?'

'From your perspective, yes. I am the creator, of your planet and of you. I am well described in the loving aspect of many of your religions, and I understand and love everything that you are and do. I know the secrets of every heart and I forgive everything because I am you, through the function of my photons. You need only relax and you will feel my love all around you and within you. Not a fly dies without my knowledge, without my care.

'And yet, from my perspective, I am not God, but a channel for God or Source's love, as it fills the universe, the galaxies, the constellations and the star systems. I focus this love into your world. Now, let me explain that it is a not a hierarchy which structures these aspects of Source. It is merely a question of time, that because time exists in this universe, things change and move on. Now I am one of so many stars in this universe that the number surpasses the grains of sands on all your beaches, below all your oceans. I change, from your perspective, with solar flares and storms and eventually will become a red giant, then to collapse into a white dwarf. From my perspective, I will have finished my work here in this planetary system, and will grow in immensity before eventually finding my way to the phenomenon of the so called black hole. These 'black holes' are more like wormholes, and all of them connect ultimately with the black hole in the centre of the Milky Way, so that I become one with the mind of the galaxy. Over time, the rest of my constellation, the Chalice, will do the same. Many others from the Chalice are already there. In the central 'black hole' our consciousnesses are woven together with that of the galaxy, and with all the other star systems that find their way there, so that we can become one vast, glorious, galactic group mind.

'These minds are all nested one within the other. This is the holographic aspect of this universe. Source holds, and indeed creates, all the billions of universes. This universe holds us all, the galaxies hold us all, the constellations hold us all, I hold us all. And you hold us all. Within you, individually, is the ability to experience the Diamond Light of the galaxies and the Diamond Luminosity of the universe. Your brains have a vast number of connections which are illuminated when your heart is opened, and can then encompass these powerful states. Your serious meditators and psychonauts and those souls occasionally blessed with profound grace can experience this beautiful clarity. You can see it in the art of other times, portraying saints and Jesus and Bodhisattvas and Buddhas with halos. A halo shows the light of the Sun within, made visible in the light around the person. It is interesting how many spiritual books, artifacts, YouTube talks etc focus on light, illustrating it often with pictures of me, knowing and trusting that the light is all, without looking out of the window and seeing the living reality of this!

'When you practise awareness and empty your mind of thought, you begin to be in touch with my light on the existence of everything, and with Source, which is ultimate light and love. This is how all is one. You are as much the universe as much as you are an individual, as much as you are a grain of sand, truly holographic. As above, so below, as Hermes Trismegistus says. There is no separation, there is only love and that is what unites us all.

'In your beauty, your love, your compassion, you are the eternal and infinite Source. Divine. Holy. The Creator.

'In your ugliness, your hatred, your selfishness, you are the eternal and infinite Source. Divine. Holy. The Creator.

'Can you believe this? If you cannot, you are limiting the Creator, or your idea of God. You are effectively saying that the love that fills the universes is unable to tolerate a part of itself, that it is less than perfect. A nonsense. You, and I, and all those billions of stars, the galaxies and all those universes are ideas in Source's consciousness. We are all part of the imagination/ creativity/ emanation of Source. Therefore, nothing is imperfect, nothing is wrong, or failing. You are perfect, nothing you do is wrong, nothing will fail.'

'What is free will then? If nothing is wrong? What is the point of it?'

'Source has but one state. It is the serene beauty of being, the clarity and purity, the state of perfect love and light in the eternal moment, which we can all access when we are aware. This is the truth of who we are, expansive, transparent, timeless and at one. And then, something happens. This is why there's a Big Bang or whatever you want to call it. The moment of creation. It's the nature of love to give, to overflow. Love is a verb as well as a noun and so is light. It's the nature of light to shine. It must shine on something. There must be something to give to. The active state of love, overflowing, which is creativity, sets time going and then the universes can start taking place. And everything starts to happen. This is about coming out to play. This is Source's magnificent game, and it works because of what happens next. This is about the flow of time, wherein all the universes are created.

'And because the moment changes, the beings within these successive moments have to dance along this flow of time, loving and losing. The change of one moment to another means that there is free will because we live in time. If there is change, from one moment to the next, free will is exercised, just as Source exercised freewill, Divine Will, in getting time going.

'For you, thinking about time is mandatory because you need to understand the workings of cause and effect. If I do this, then that. If I do that, then this. Fear, anxiety, dread, anticipation,

hope, of the future; regret, nostalgia, guilt, mourning for the past...
all become the bedrock of your inner chatter. I did that, and this
happened. This is how karma works, this is freewill, and this is
the karmic context. The serpent, tempting Eve with the apple,
said that she and Adam would become gods, if they ate it. They
were, of course already gods, but had never realised it. Eat this,
said the serpent. You will know much more and there will be a
change. And indeed, in that story, there was change. It was called
knowledge, the knowledge of good and evil. Before that change,
there was awareness, innocence, clarity, love, the infinite state of
Source in an eternal moment, union with the Divine. Afterwards,
separation, the polarities, good and evil, male and female, black
and white, day and night. And there we have it, the pain and
suffering, karmic consequences, and the whole wheel of samsara
begins to turn, as your ego minds get going. This is only one of
many stories, all of them metaphors, but it gives the essence.

'The banishment from Eden is a metaphor for the veil. The veil is
a function of sequential time. And you may rage at me for this.
Many have hated God, blamed God, because of the intolerable
degree of suffering. And you may think that I have not given
enough weight to the sheer horror of, for example, the Holocaust,
of the deaths of children, of famine, war, torture. Violation, rape,
sadism. This is the essence, the point where the spiritual and
mystic usually fall down. But I have been there. I was with you
in Auschwitz and Belsen. I tried to feed my starving infant with
empty breasts. I felt my bones stretch apart from the flesh on the

rack. I burned at the stake. I hung on the cross. I know what it is like and it is indeed terrible. Grinding and vicious pain, horror and despair. Fear. The victims' role is one to be abhorred.

'Yet I was also the rapist, the torturer, the soldier, the Nazi. Why did they do it? How could they do it? Such people, the perpetrators, are at the far end of the spectrum between separation and unity. They have been so damaged by their environment and context that they are cut off from their victims' suffering. They have no empathy, no compassion or love. They could not do the terrible things they did if they were not cut off. It's called denial, denial of who we really are.

'The walls of denial are built high, and strengthened by pain. This is the case for both perpetrator and victim. This is the most profound of catalytic encounters. Just a minute step away from separation might enable the seed of compassion to grow for the perpetrator. Just one tiny instant of understanding, might begin to transform the agony for the victim, because an appreciation of the bigger picture is the seed of grace. It is all about perspective, perception, for both of them. And it is the most serious of questions, whether in that moment, that appalling moment, the seed can be recognised. And so this is also the most crucial moment of free will. What will the victim or perpetrator do? Will the Nazi guard find enough inner strength to say no, when he knows he and his family might finish up with the people he is about to murder? Will the victim, on the way to the gas oven, be able to remember that this is only one life, a tiny fragment of experience, when she's wondering where her child is, who may also die?

'Compassion is all, all you can give, all you can do, whichever way it goes. Your families bring you to your knees. This is the family connection, the deep-seated, instinctual part of you. It is the fabric of your being, written into your DNA, that your family is your home, your safety, your security. At least, it should be. Divorce, break up, poverty, war, mental and physical illness, many things can destroy the feeling of safety. For that is what you all want, what you try to replicate for your own children. In war and famine, it is taken out of your hands. You cannot keep your family safe, no matter what. At this deep level, fear takes over. Fear is always waiting there, ready to pull you away from love. It's there because you love, because you are a warm-blooded animal who needs to keep its young safe. This is what fuels the movement of refugees, risking anything, to keep the family safe. Another sharp edge to the veil, that the opposite of love is not hate, but fear.

'From the births of your children, if all goes well, the love you feel for them is, for most people, probably the strongest emotion of your lives. You will do anything for them, run into burning houses, jump into freezing lakes, dole out all your money, travel the countryside, get up night after night, after night, because they cry. The identifiable mechanism for this is the flood of oxytocin at birth, which bonds most parents and infants for their lifetimes.

In evolutionary terms, it's necessary because human babies are singularly ill equipped to look after themselves for many years. There needs to be a way to ensure they will be looked after and that's what the loving, protective side of parental love does. And in most cases it long outlives its evolutionary role and lasts instead, a lifetime.

'When your children suffer, most of you wish you could take the suffering from them, and do it for them. You become wild with hatred and fury if anyone damages or causes hurt to your child. You also sometimes, horribly, guiltily, wish they had never been born. Your worry, your stress, your weariness sometimes makes you long for the state before their birth. They exhaust you, press your buttons, and drive you hard up to the end boundary of what you can tolerate. Sometimes they will not let you keep them safe. This shows you how close hatred is to love, too. It can sometimes feel as if they have ruined your life. Your deepest role, as a parent, is to keep your children safe. And when you cannot, who do you blame? It's comparatively easy if there's an obvious enemy, in war or famine. If there's disease too, you can blame that. But when it's only the family, and the children don't obey, won't listen, dice with drugs or drink, join gangs, drop out of school or college, or become promiscuous, do you blame them, or yourself?

'You brought them up. And this will point out your frailties, your ambivalence, your self-love, your guilt and so much else. It's via your children that catalyst can most affect you. This is the deep instinctual level that traps so many of you. Even if you don't have children, you were one once yourself, and you will know what you thought about your family. Even if it was a failing family, you will know what you wanted. Two loving parents, enough to eat and drink, the right clothes for the season and so on. We all understand this dynamic. It lies behind our formation of society, our need for health care, education, housing, the legal system, for taxes to fund these things, for administrators and politicians, to help us keep our families safe. We work ourselves to the bone, to give our children what they need and often too, what they want.

'Feeling this depth of passion for your child can also enable a similar understanding of the complicated love that other parents experience. They all do. And so which of you, childless and parents alike, was not shaken by that picture on the beach, of the father carrying his dead child after a refugee boat had sunk? This is the catalyst at work again, drawing you together in compassion.

'Incidentally, this is why the institutions of monasticism, the celibacy of so many priesthoods, often appear inadequate, especially if they take the moral high ground with people's sexuality and family life. They are perhaps aware that the exigencies of family life are a distraction from the holy life. They see prayer or meditation as the way through the veil and they are not wrong. These methods can work, over time. But having a family, bringing up children, or working in hospitals or the social services, is a quicker route to understanding. This is the coal face to the veil, the hardest of challenges, the most vicious aspects of catalyst. They do not and cannot know the most powerful catalytic functions in this incarnation, although they have very probably experienced them in previous lifetimes, which is why they have chosen the contemplative life this time round.

'And yet I say, remember that the veil is lifted through grace. And grace is woven into suffering, it is always available. Suffering rips you open to grace. Just as Matte Blanco, the psychoanalyst who realised how your minds work, explained, to reach the depths, the essence of who you are, you often have to go through emotion, through your despair, grief, agony, to find the seed of compassion, the fragment of knowledge of who you really are. It is always there. I am always there, with you. And so love is always there, no matter how deeply buried. Forgiveness is the trump card in this game, forgiveness for self and others. As parents you will always fail. It is impossible to get it right all of the time. And yet you do your best, exhausted, stressed and worried though you may be: self compassion, self forgiveness is of the essence.

'Of course the stars, their constellations and the galaxies are caught in time too, but we have learned the lessons of suffering long ago and although we do indeed change, it is not due to karmic consequences. It is instead about celebration. And as I have said, our time is different to yours, not sequential in the same way.

'Free will still has to be understood. Any decision that you take is the result of your experiences up to that point, including your genetic inheritance. There is a complicated web of memories, emotions, predispositions and habits that influences any decision you may make. Thus it may appear as if there is no free will, and in one way that is the truth. You are, at any one point in time, the result of your genetic, astrological and lifetime experiences. For a decision to have karmic consequences, you must deliberately behave in a certain fashion, cruelly or kindly, and know what you are doing. You must mean it. The things you do without thought, no matter how terrible, are accidents or mistakes and do not have karmic consequences. However, some people (Freud, for example) say there are no accidents or mistakes, and that is, in a way, also true. These thoughtless, unprepared events come from the unconscious; that is, from the deeper parts of the self, the soul or Higher Self, if you like, and are lessons, available to you if you wish, functions of grace, that is all. They are grace because they unite you with everyone else. Because all of you make mistakes, all of you are occasionally thoughtless, and all of you can be carelessly cruel or destructive at times.

'If you are thoughtful enough afterwards to realise that you have been cruel, you can see that other people may be thoughtless when they are being cruel. If they were being deliberately cruel, there will be karmic consequences; there is nothing you need do, except get out of the way! If you were being thoughtless, you can think how to do better next time, perhaps even develop a strategy. And then forgiveness can arise, for self and for everyone else. There are no exceptions. This is one of the many associations between freewill and creativity. Forgiveness is about being creative. It's making things better, loosening the chains of blame and recrimination. It's putting harmony back into mix.

'Forgiveness is the answer, for yourself and for everyone. Freewill is a function of time because it's about actions and consequences. This is why the game in third density is so endlessly fascinating, for yourselves, for the stars, the galaxies and the universes. And Source. There is freewill, and therefore suffering. There is the option of forgiveness. Will they or won't they? Keep going round or releasing the chains of blame, victimhood, revenge? These are the great stories, the myths of redemption. This is why it all happens, as it happens.

'But when you are in the moment, in the presence of the eternal beingness in joy and love, there is no time. No past or future. No consequences or regrets. And therefore, no narrative and no freewill.'

Chapter 6   Gaia

*****

'I'd like to explain to you more about the densities, especially the first three. This will put you even more into the context of this universe and help you understand the bigger picture.

'As you are in third density, you have behind you a multitude of incarnations in first and second densities. You have already come a very long way! And third density takes place over millions of years. Some of you have taken many incarnations within it already, those you call 'old souls' and those are nearing the transition into fourth density. Others are still young souls, closer in time to second density.

'Your scientists conceive of the formation of galaxies and star systems as the result of gravity, that vast nebulas of gases gradually coalesce, or condense down into rocky substances, which then coalesce into stars and planets.

'They are not far wrong. Gravity is a part of love. It draws things together. In this universe, in this particular dream from Source, everything is pulling together, being created, taking form through gravity/love, at the same time as it is expanding. This is a dynamic tension, how gravity holds steady against the expansion. From the quantum level to the galaxies, things stay in relation to each other as matter, and matter, all of it, is the result of love. The delight in being together.   Matter is the same word, etymologically speaking, as mother. This is about the love of the Great Mother, our galaxy, in the making of her children, and how her children joyfully progress towards her.

'I was created within the Milky Way galaxy, in the first of a thousand densities of incarnations I have experienced. Over time, ever growing, I joined together with others in ever wider group consciousnesses. From my perspective, these were the upper stages of going through densities. From your perspective I would look like a swirling cloud of gases, something you call a nebula or a star nursery.   This is the wide spread of a vast group consciousness, spanning other dimensions as well as this one. Eventually it would seem that the time is right, that we have enough understanding and love to start our own solar system. So, over millions of your years we settled into a proto-star, which is from your perspective an almost flat disk, beginning to feel our way into beingness in matter. We get closer and closer together, our love spanning the trillions of smaller group minds, spanning so many different lives and experiences, universe wide experiences, intensely delighting in each other, intensely loving, excited about this project, which again through millions of your years becomes a sphere, or a star. This is how we burst into radiance. This is who I am. This is who you are, too. This is why I tell you that you span galaxies, you contain not only all this world but countless others too. Your understanding is universe wide. You are God, as I am.

'The experience of those times I treasure, the deep joy of beingness in the beautiful creative heart of the Mother, our Milky Way galaxy was inexpressibly heart-opening, full of glory, full of wonder and the most tender of lovingness. It was cross-dimensional in many respects, as the looser structures of gas clouds and nebula are, and gave me the experience of existences of which you cannot even dream. They are part of me now, together with all those other group minds that have joined me here. We are one, and also diverse, as you are.

'Then I, the multiple creative being that I am, inescapably creative, as indeed you are, too, embarked in the great project of starting off a solar system. And I must tell you that Gaia was not the first of our essays into planet formation in this system. But here I will deal with Gaia, because you will relate much more easily to this.

'You have the first three, exquisitely precious densities behind you, where you are now on Gaia. This is how matter, the great generous act of Source, to give us the Great Mother, matter progresses, being filled gradually with light and love until it is Source again.'

'It sounds circular, as if everything is just going round in circles....vast circles, eons in time, but still circles.'

'Yes, almost right. But it's a spiral rather than a circle, an endless spiral in time.'

'Where does the spiral get to?'

'Ultimately to Source, to the unweaving of time and space. The spiral structures much of space/time. Many galaxies, like the Milky Way, are spiral shaped.'

'So it is still circular. We set off through the densities, there's all this suffering, in order to get back where we started!'

'Back where you started with the loveliness of what you have passed through. You and I are augmented by what we have experienced. You are not the same as you were when you started. You are not the same as you were when you were born this time around, even not the same as you were when you got up today. It's all a journey. The universe becomes more glorious, richer with experience, more beautiful, deeper with love, because of what we have experienced. This is why there's something, rather than nothing.'

It's another joke. I hear the soft laughter again, echoing everywhere. It's in the bare branches of trees, in the golden hearts of daffodils outside, in the warm scent of the hyacinths by my mother's chair. It's in the deep breathing, near snoring, of the two dogs beside me. It's softer, it's kinder. More gentle. So beautiful.

'The planets are the children of my heart,' says the Sun. 'I, all the billions of souls who compose who I am, I imagined what would happen. Think of the resources we could bring to this! I am a universe wide intelligence. I held our ideas in place within my infinite intelligence and through the process of imagination/creativity/emanation we elaborated how it would go, adding land masses, gases, climates, and everything that you are.

'You here, the gorgeous Gaia, started as a burning, volcanic sphere, streaming lava, gas....this is first density and it was such fun, such a delight to get this going! This was me as Gaia, celebrating with such glorious excitement that the great progression was underway! It was champagne fizzy, in your terms. Other stars in the Chalice sent matter in the shape of meteors to join the party, and one particular rather large meteorite became your moon. Your scientists know it as Theia. This was a gift from Aldebaran, who has a particular connection with Gaia. Your moon is thus a special visitor to this system, bringing Aldebaran energies to the environment here. More about that later.

'I am Gaia, but at this point I expanded the perspective so that she could have creative freewill, in the genesis of her being. This is how it all works. Such an adventure this is! From the heat of the volcanoes, we had Ice Ages, which you call 'Snowball Planet', when even the oceans froze! Those were beautiful times, and we became the great silences of the vast snow fields which were whipped into wild dances in the howling winds. There were massive snow mountains, glaciers, huge icebergs rising out of the freezing ocean, sparkling with joy! These were magnificent playgrounds! We had visitors from throughout the Chalice, those in vibrational modes, to join us in these celebrations. These Ice Ages will come again.'

'But does life survive these great freezes?'

'Life does, always. Everything is Source, everything. Everything is the dream of consciousness, everything lives in this dream. But few species... some in the deepest ocean, some in the cooling volcanoes. But you must realise that nearly all species are what you call extinct. Something like 99% have become extinct during the history of Gaia. You have only documented a tiny proportion of the species on Gaia now, and have hardly noticed as so many disappear. Beetles, rodents, birds, fish... there are millions of species unknown by your scientists. It doesn't matter. Those that are extinct return to me. And reincarnate. You yourselves have been extinct many times, as you travelled through the first two densities.

'We – Gaia and myself – arranged for varieties of gas to combine, until oxygen began to appear, and water, the great oceans, and we became ready to create life, getting ready for animal life. We began with a single cell life and we imagined together how to develop this. With joy, we engineered multi-celled life, weaving into each cell the strand of DNA which would eventually direct the form the individual would take. The great game is moved on by what you call epigenetics, the interrelation of DNA and the outside world. Evolution, if you like. This was much informed by the more powerful photons, giving the potential for consciousness of various levels. Of course, all of Gaia is made of photons from my imaginative world combined with the other particles you're familiar with.'

'And thus we come to second density. Those parts of us that had been the mountains, volcanoes, icebergs, water and either stay there or move on to second density, as we wish. Second density is the kind of life that can move around, can turn towards the Sun or not. So this is plants, trees, and animals, including birds, reptiles, insects. At every point, in every density, parts of me can elect to stay where they are, or move on.'

'This is true for many of you now, where you are in third density. You can stay in third density, or move on. The beauty of compassion... It's the Bodhisattva vow. With your awareness of the difficulties here, will you move on and leave others behind here? With your understanding of the veil and what is going on, should you perhaps take another few incarnations until we can make sure that everyone can become fourth density?'

'But won't they all get there in the end? Whether we incarnate again or not?'

'Yes! This is fifth density thinking. Fourth always wants to help, will martyr itself in the sometimes fruitless desire to help others... such was the dilemma of my greatly beloved self known widely as Jesus Christ. Love and compassion must be tempered by wisdom and light!

'It will be useful here to think about energy. I have told you that you are energy and that so is everything around you. And this was true of the times before third density. The vibrational form takes flesh, in species, creatures, and continues the vibrational patterns of first density. Therefore the more active volcanoes might eventually become the very speedy dinosaurs, the ones who could run fast, high on their two legs, whereas the big land masses might have become the great slow moving plant eaters. These are the energies behind you now. There was savagery in some dinosaurs, placidity in others. Their reign on Gaia was for more than 160 million of your years, and makes the appearance of humanity on this planet look very transient, being much less than one million. But of course, there was plenty of time for the dinosaurs to reincarnate repeatedly, gradually evolving until the vibrational, energetic part of them could become part of conventional mammals, fish, insects, and most importantly, birds.

'Thus we come to the splits, the dualities which apparently influence you so much. And now I must explain to you the yin/yang symbol I showed you, a while back. You could look at the world as it is now, and seemingly identify the savage and the cruel. Your history is full of monsters. And it is true that souls such as the Hitler soul are much influenced by a raptor past. And you could think, then is it like the old story, the scorpion who asks the frog to carry it across the river. The frog is reluctant; 'What if you sting me?' it asks.

The scorpion says, 'Why would I? We'd both drown.'

This seems sensible so the frog agrees. Half way across the scorpion stings the frog and they realise they're both going to die. But as they start to drown, the frog asks, 'Why did you sting me?

The scorpion replies, 'It's my nature.'

'Am I saying, then, that the monsters of this world – Adolf Hitler, Gilles de Rais, Pol Pot, Fred West, Joseph Stalin, the slave traders, and so many others - have an inescapable nature, left over from this deep past? No. This is the crucial difference between second and third density. There is a self awareness in third density entirely missing from the ages of the dinosaurs. Self-awareness and freewill. But the monsters are up against it! They may have chosen human incarnations to allow these savage energies one last fling, and having done so, will, with self-awareness, realise that guilt will have its place. Remorse, shame, self-hatred, despair will become constant companions to such a soul. It will have to incarnate again and again, to exorcise the terrible things it did. This is the tiny white circle in the black part of the yin-yang symbol.

'There is another consequence for the third density from the age of the dinosaurs. It is that of duality, from that splitting of the savage from the placid. You can see it in Greek thinking, the split between Apollo and Dionysius, and another split, which I now wish to explain, between the Sun and the Moon.

'You have a difficulty in seeing me as beyond male and female. In your thoughts, I am often masculine. This may be a consequence of being brought up in a vaguely Christian society, and it may be the consequence of my overwhelming physical power, which you as a woman of your age, have tended to see as a masculine prerogative. Because of this power in the equatorial religions of the Egyptians and the Central Americas, I am often portrayed as a savage god, a masculine god, in need of sacrifice and placating in every way they could think. And my heat and light is extreme in these regions and is so, to encourage you to take care, to learn how to protect yourselves, how to use my fierce power. And yet, I am often portrayed as a cruel, exacting god, the opposite of the soft warm, gentle light of the moon. She is often portrayed maternal, feminine, sometimes hidden and tricksy, mysterious. Nowhere near so powerful. And both of us are misread in these portrayals.

'You and the rest of humanity look at the surface, the obvious. You are bamboozled by your public figures because they appear to be strongly one thing or another. You often do not trouble to look deeper. You do not see the frightened child inside, desperately trying to impress a neglectful parent by becoming powerful, which is behind so many of your leaders. That is a more frequent path than you might imagine. You do not look at the beggar in the street and bother to find out where they come from. A successful business man who lost his job, a courageous soldier who was traumatised, someone using drugs to deaden a tragic loss, someone who being dyslexic never managed to work?

'In loving my light, looking at the blazing sky at sunset, looking at the sunburn on your arm, you do not remember my gentleness, the softness of my light in northern climes or at twilight. My warmth moving through the hard winter soil is gentle, a thawing, a melting of hardness. I bathe you in kindness, in the sweetness of good things; I am maternal in your care while I am paternal in your care too. I am both, I am all, and if you in this incarnation identify so much as in your role as a mother, I am as much a mother as you are and much more so. But really I am way beyond male and female, something else beyond simple heterosexuality, which is a fairly common method of reproduction throughout the Universe. Not as common as hermaphroditism. Or even parthenogenesis. For I have been through all forms of reproduction and sexuality, throughout all different climates and times, in other Star systems far from this one. It amuses me, your insistence that because I seem powerful and you remember your mythologies, I must be male!'

And so it is. When I talk about Sol I very often, by mistake, call it 'he'.

'The Moon too is characterised as soft and gentle... yet, look to your mythologies again. The huntress Artemis was a Moon goddess. She has arrows, she shoots, and moon light can pierce you to the heart with its clarity, changing you unalterably. The Moon comes from Aldebaran, the great red giant which is home to the ideal, the archetype of Epiphany, the sudden shock, the jolt that moves one on. This is power, this is the transformative aspect of the Moon you so often miss. It has a huge role in your history, from Paul on the road to Damascus, to your own small but no less dramatic epiphanies.'

And often, atheist though I was, I want to give praise for the sheer beauty of the Sun's being, the sheer beauty of the silver Moon, the sheer beauty of Gaia now, in the burgeoning springtime. It's myself, I remember, and sometimes feel a vast glory, something that seems much wider than this mere physical frame. I am the Sun, I feel. I am Gaia. I am everyone.

So are you, reading this, with these manifest enchantments round you. Is it not a miracle?

Chapter 7   Why it is so difficult here? Part 2

'We have thought about the Universe, how time structures everything therein. We have thought about Source, existing in an eternal, perfect, clear eternity of light and love.

'Now, you are an immortal soul and you are not only in touch with Source, you are Source, you are Divine, and you have an inner shining, which is my light and which is also the light of Source. This is the real you, at one with everything, timeless and eternal. You are Source. Know this. And yet you live in this Universe as a separate being, and are subject to time. To cope with life, the separate you must have a narrative self, a stream of inner talking that keeps you going, reminding you, if you are a fortunate middle-class person in a western country, to walk the dogs, fetch the grandchild from school, pay the bill, send that email, put on the potatoes, arrange a Zoom meeting, phone the friend, finish that book, prune the roses. You wonder why your friend hasn't rung; did you offend her when you met last week? You're aware you ate too much at breakfast, and the dress you want to wear at the weekend will be no nearer to fitting. You worry about the gathering at the weekend, will that couple be there who got so drunk, will it be that ghastly New Age music, and vegan nibbles? Will your partner behave and not want to go home early? What will happen to the Labour Party now? Should you resign?

'What will happen to your job if the Coronavirus lockdown goes on? How will you pay the bills, when it's already a stretch? Your elderly mother needs attending too, taking to the hairdressers and what to give her for lunch. Why is she always so needy? Can you fit that in? And oh yes, when is that man coming to point the mortar on the chimney? Your brother's birthday! The car needs an MOT, and it's doubtful it will pass. All the fuss of finding a new car, will we have to? There's Christmas up ahead and a vast family to buy for, and the food to arrange.

'It never stops. Yes, it's all very ordinary, everyday catalyst, but it still needs attending to and there are not enough hours in the day, and even as in your case, you are retired and your children live elsewhere. How can someone who works, who has young children, manage? How can you recognise the loving, light-filled soul within when the narrative self has to go rushing on? This is what the psychologists call the default mode network. We slip into it all the time. Few of you can spend the luxury of an hour a day meditating. But very occasionally, you can just pause, wait for a moment in silence, and stay in the moment. Let the thoughts go... you may have made a list, so you don't have to keep trying to remember everything, but even if not, a few seconds 'off', just a moment or two of peace and quiet, and nothing will go wrong, and you will begin to know who you really are. Breathe into it. Three breaths are enough. You are not your thoughts. They are a construct which gets going in infancy, to help you manage the external world. But they are not who you are. Your thoughts are not who you are... remember this. It bears contemplation.

'Just as pain divorces you from the external world, you too can switch off from it and open up your senses to the truth of who you are, to the reality of unity. Everything is contained in awareness and when you are aware of awareness, you can begin to sense the soul within and without, the Source within and without. Your Sun, inside and outside, through the window.

'It's a vast project, getting to know Source. All these universes, all these centillions of stars and galaxies, all those dimensions without stars and with something unimaginable instead, those others without time/space, without light, only love, or without love and only light. There are different colours elsewhere, different physical laws, different geometries and biologies and mathematics, all beyond your imaginations. Just as Source is infinitely creative, so our play within creation is unlimited. Delight, Celebration and Rapture run through Creation, boundlessly laughing with joy.'

'I feel so joyful; I don't know what to do with it. If I feel gratitude, you say I'm thanking myself!'

'Isn't it a grand joke?'

'The best!'

'Relax and enjoy Divine Will, which is that Creation is bursting with florescence and liveliness and laughter! Like a parent throwing a child into the air, always catching their darling so safely, so I throw you out into your lives, and catch you safely as you come home to me.'

'What happens after death?'

'You return to me, to the powerful energy of my being. My photons are, in third density, entwined with the electrons and quarks and protons to make you and all matter and the air all around you. When you die, the photons which are your divine self leave their relationship with electrons and others and start the journey home. It sometimes takes up to eight of your minutes for the photons to arrive here. That is the dark tunnel described in so many of your near-death experiences. Sometimes it's instantaneous. Some souls need a little time to unwind after the stress of a third density life and there is healing for them. But within me you will experience the original beauty of my creativity in the Platonic ideal of your world. You see it in its true colours, alive with light and vibrating with love. You will hear the truth of music, in the vibration of everything, the harmony of every leaf, every blade of grass in the fair landscapes you will find there. You will meet again your loved ones, and your unloved ones, and will recognise that you are all one. You will decide eventually to reincarnate together, or not. If the time is right you will join many others in what Ra rightly calls 'The Harvest' and be released from third density. You will progress towards fourth density, where love and compassion are everything. You may find Jesus there, and many of your saints and holy people, gurus and bodhisattvas.'

'What happens to fourth density beings?'

'They can reincarnate until they progress towards fifth density.'

'Is that within you too?'

'Yes, but as I am intelligent infinity, as is everything created in Source, fourth and fifth density beings can go anywhere to reincarnate, to any of the planets in this system, or to any in the other solar systems in this constellation. Sixth density is generally based on the planet you call Saturn, and seventh density is on Jupiter. The eighth density (or first density of the next octave), generally takes place on another star within the Chalice, Aldebaran, which is a vast red giant. Its structures are looser, less intense than my own, and can more easily span other dimensions. That is why it happily takes on board further octaves than your own. Third density flourishes within intensity. It's powerful, isn't it, here? But localised, narrow focused. The further densities and octaves are thus all spread around within this corner of our galaxy, the Milky Way, generally in the older stars.'

'How do the beings travel to such distant stars?'

'The distances are not far to us, because travel takes place through im/cre/em, instantaneously. We imagine where we want to be, create an imagined pathway and then emanate there. It happens within a moment, the moment, the timeless present we experience in awareness. We become one with the creative aspect of Source with our im/cre/em, and travel is simultaneous with imaginative thought.'

'What happens to us as individuals after death?'

'Having traversed the tunnel into the light, you will find yourself in the astral plain, which is much influenced by your own imaginations. You may find that there is still be work to be done, but eventually, your personality and memories begin to fade into unimportance, and the essence of you, your uniquely loving vibration, will be reunited with other vibrations with whom you have reincarnated so often. This is your soul group. You celebrate being back together, you dance and twirl in energetic patterns together and eventually may decide to take another reincarnation, or not, as you like. There may be a consciousness of something left undone, and that may call you to reincarnate on Gaia.'

'Has it always been like that?'

'That is certainly why my darling children reincarnate, and have done so countless times.'

'What kinds of things are left undone?'

'It's always about your relationship with others, and how far you've managed to love them and see them as parts of yourself. How far you've gone in forgiveness, how far you've gone in love. If you are clinging to separate ideas of others, there is still work to be done.'

'That's really hard. Even if I understand it intellectually, there the others are, all doing their own thing, all essentially themselves.'

'And all, essentially, you. Drop the intellect, forget that. That's your narrative self. Think with your emotions, your heart, think how much they suffer, they try, laugh and cry and love and make messes and are you. You can understand this, can you not, with your heart?'

'That certainly helps... but I'm still a long way from really feeling they're the same as me.'

'They are not really the same. You are diverse. But you are all made of the same stuff in its infinite variety, your very diversity springs from the same Source. You are the same family, more than a family, you are like the fingers on a hand. Each different, but so linked, and if you could really embrace this, it would be impossible to be unkind, cruel or violent. Could your thumb suddenly take against your ring finger? It's ridiculous.

'Think, too, about what a wonderful star you will all make. With all these aeons of experience, all those deaths, all those births, all those individual lifetimes in between. The poet, the farmer, the beggar, the queen... and all those ordinary people, just pegging away at their work, paying the bills, bringing up kids, having sex, watching TV, playing with their phones, eating food. Courageously keeping going, 'rolling with the punches', as you might say, as catalyst throws up one dilemma after another. All those experiences, all, will go into the mix of the star you will all become.

'That is why so many insights, in books, films, workshops, ceremonies, are about vitality. About liveliness, going for it, in life, relishing what you've been given, loving and living and losing and doing it all. It all enriches the group mind.'

'What about the recluses, the monks and nuns who stay locked away, not apparently doing anything much?'

'Your star will need a quieter, more contemplative side of course... There is nothing that you do that is unacceptable. All the actions you judge to be harmful are always about separation, and that is what the third density is about. So as you move towards the magnificent star you will become, all those separate mistakes will drop away with increasing forgiveness and compassion.'

'That seems very far away.'

'Once you are beyond third density, once you know who you are and what the pathways are, you will live in joy almost all of the time. The lengths of time it takes to move towards being a star, countless millennia, will pass in graceful measure, aeons upon aeons, and you will be bathed in the beauty of love for all of it. You will be in bliss, in heaven if you like, but with a knowledge of movement, progression. No static fields of lilies filled with angels singing my praises! Knowing you are one with me, you dance down the timelines.

'You may deep down have that knowledge here and now. Some of you know this. And there's so much you can do now, to make it feel better, when you are creative, when you are forgiving.

'Another thought is to try to remember when you talk to anyone or have any contact with another, that you are talking to me, making contact with me. Our dear self Neale Donald Walsch puts it well: 'There I go again!' when you see the homeless, the drunk, the beggar, the thief. I am looking at you through everyone else's eyes. I am you, looking at them. This is the literal truth, because you are everyone and you are me. And there you go again. And I am everywhere, everything, everybody.'

'That's rather like making everything you do an act of love.'

'Yes, indeed it is. Transform your world into a theatre of love. Interpret everything everyone does as an act of love. Try it for a few minutes, try it for an hour. Think of those people around you, whatever they're doing as acting out love. Even if they're shouting, crashing around, weeping, try to see the love behind it. Are they wounded, suffering, acting out because of the pressures inside? How can that be love? They're wounded because they are not understood, they want to communicate, get close to others, but others do not understand. So they shout and complain or weep in despair. Some shut themselves off with alcohol, or even reading can keep you isolated. Think of those locked into their gaming machines, cut off and separate from you. Is that love? Perhaps the stress of getting close is too difficult, too conflictual. They are often working with avatars, achieving something, making something and even though it's second hand, they are safely negotiating one of the trials of third density and resting, relaxing, taking a break from the conflict, at the same time. There's love in that, for self, to be sure, but love nonetheless. But like any activity, if it becomes addictive, then you are trapped, closing the walls round yourself and wilfully locking the door. You are sinking into third density distraction, and far removed from who you are. Addiction, of whatever kind, distracts us from the pain of separation. That is its power.

'It's all the longing of love to become close together. Our dear self Rupert Spira says 'Love is the end of relationship; it is the revelation of our shared being.' Another dear self Peter Deunov said, 'Leave everything to love. It will put everything right.' This is right. This is the answer. But you need to try it out, as I said, transform your world, your actions and those of everyone else into a theatre for love. And play hide and seek, try to find the love in everything. It's easy in the natural world, which is why it's such a relief to get out there in the fields and woods and beaches and sea sides. It is manifestly so beautiful that love clearly comes shining through.

'But in town and cities, in slums, and tower blocks, the boredom of suburbia, shopping malls and factories, traffic jams and airport queues, how is that love? It is love in the way people struggle to survive, in the way they endeavour to bring home food for their families, or to cheer themselves, even if it's through drink and drugs. Think of all the weddings, the parties and anniversaries, the parties, the lunches out with friends... the meetings at the pub, the choir, the concert... At home you try to feel at one with your friends and families, but anywhere you may need drink or drugs to batten down the insecurities and self loathing that so many suffer. All of you, whatever you do, at a deep level want to be at one with each other and your incredible creativity in setting up scenarios for this is such a delight!'

'The virus has separated us.'

'It is showing you what you value, putting it out on the table. Do your possessions matter? Do your meals out, your visits to the gym, the cinema, your holidays, your new cars, new dress, any of it matter, besides not being able to hug your children? Not being able to visit your elderly mother in her care home? Not to be with your beloved father, son, wife, friend as they die? What do you actually care about? It could not be clearer. The difficulty of staying apart is a catalytic lesson in what you value, and in separation. It feels wrong, doesn't it? At Christmas, those congregations not allowed to sing. Those football matches played without crowds to cheer them along. It feels deeply aberrant, doesn't it? You were created to sing and cheer together. You were created to laugh, and yet even that may spread the infection. You cannot even see each other smile, wearing a mask.

'You are social animals, designedly so. But this is throwing you back on yourselves, back into the narrative of who you are. And is it enough? Don't you need the others to make sense of it?'

'Oh, yes, indeed! I'd heard that we're all locked down with the people we have karma with, as if it's pushing us into sorting it out, somehow or other. And if we're on our own, it's ourselves we need to focus on.'

'Yes, lovely, but it sounds a bit punitive like that. The virus is love, too. Nothing is outside love. It is a loving working out of karma for many people, even though it is dangerous.   Necessary karmically driven catalyst. You might, perhaps dwell on that, as well as this strange Christmas which has been so difficult for many. There is no end to love, no end to its incredible creativity in making the next moment.'

Chapter 8   Consciousness and Love

The material I received from the Sun so far is all so thought provoking that I have decided to explore, consider and contemplate further what it means.

'You are in my heart.'

This first direct communication points to the significance of emotion in spiritual experiences. It was the sheer warmth of the love that took me by surprise. It melted my heart in gratitude and joy. It opened me to the most thrilling conversation of my life.

It was the grief for my father that gave me my first experience of unity consciousness and set me on a quest to understand what it meant. Without this, I would not have written my first fiction book, *Fly By Night*, which is about the necessity of accepting death. It was about a god, holding time still, so that he could love a human woman forever, without her aging or dying. But time standing still means no creativity, no new life, stagnation and this set up the conflict in the plot. I wrote it as a romp, but see now that it was a forerunner to this, this exploration of love and loss.

For it is grief, sorrow, fear and depression that can lead people to seeking, to trying to find an answer; meaning. It was when Siddhartha escaped his palace, and saw suffering, disease, cruelty and old age for the first time, that he set out on his long path to become eventually the Buddha. There's a most lovely encounter on YouTube between Rupert Spira and a woman still mourning the death of her stillborn baby, twenty years earlier. He tells her, so gently, that she was 'kissed by God' in that briefest of encounters. It set her on her path to meet him, where they were during that conversation. And in my experience, it was a profound mystery that contained both joy and emotional pain that leads to the seeking. While grief and fear can open us up to help from beyond the veil, as Matte Blanco says, joy can play a part too. It is therefore the deep things that motivate us. Why do we so love the tragic in art, drama and music? From the many requiems of the classical composers to the power of the blues, I feel that music is supreme in this, and this may be why we love it so much. This is why we have been so often told to live life to the full, to love and lose, to laugh and cry. Deep emotion stops the narrative mind, diminishes the ego, and takes us to another place. This is the path perilous, rocky, difficult, and it creatively throws us off balance.

What is creativity, but a departure from what was there already? We need to be off balance, a little mad perhaps, to compose, or paint, to write or design, because we need to shut down the narrative mind. And it is deep emotion which feeds our creativity; it's called sublimity, the moving from misery to making. In certain states, we can make beauty out of our despair, as Beethoven did during his deafness. And in making, in creating, we are Source, we are doing what we are here for, acting with freewill. This is one of the most important functions of freewill, not the moral or karmic decisions so often discussed. We are choosing from potentiality before we mark the canvas with paint, the page with words, the manuscript with notes. We imagine what it might be like and then manifest it. We are at one with Source when we create.

Forgiveness is about creativity, of course, the loosening of the karmic tangles, the opportunity to move forward, make anew the relationship, to make anew the self. So creativity is about Source, this is what matters about us. In a way, it seems that creativity is the meaning of life. It makes our life better here (I'm so grateful for all the writers I've read, all the music I've heard, the pictures I've seen, the meals I've eaten, the conversations I've had, the gardens and houses, and the friends I've made) and it offers our uniqueness, our diversity, to the Universe.

From my understanding there are countless planets with third density beings struggling with the veil. But there will only be one *St Matthew Passion*, one *King Lear*, one garden in Slough made by Sandra Brown in 1972, one particularly delicious dhal that Lakshmi made for her child, one goal by Manchester United that went in that particular arc. Everything we make is unique, and valued.

Sol says to me as I write, 'I treasure the way each of you experience your lives, in the complexity and creativity of the way you respond to my invitation to this dance with time. The more individual you are, the more extraordinary you are and what you make, the more you add to the god you will eventually become.'

Yet some of us are calm, equable and rarely seem moved. These are people who make quiet successes of their lives, with gentle, subtle creativity, cooking great and ordinary meals, loving their cats or dogs, planting their window boxes, joking with their friends. You can look at the very early stages to see where this manifest resilience comes from: the conventional story is that it is genes, and the secure loving parents who express those genes, is one answer. Another answer is that they are enjoying a holiday life, a time off from the worst of the catalyst, a time to catch breath and recharge.

It is almost a cliché that many very psychic and/or enlightened people have had disrupted or traumatic childhoods. Michael Jawer suggests that the considerable amount of pruning of brain neurones that goes on in very early childhood may have been compromised by trauma. In which case, it looks like the brains of the psychic may have more neural connections, more synapses, than those of us who are more thoroughly adjusted to our everyday world. Synesthesia is an example of over-active neurones, perhaps, making connections that others don't make. Composers, like Alexander Scriabin, with a highly developed sense of synesthesia, often associate sounds with colours. But perhaps most of us, including myself, the 60% with secure attachments, are blunted by the pruning: we never see ghosts or auras, or have premonitions, or poltergeists, while those who suffered in infancy or childhood, have the additional grace of being more open to the psychic world. Another, contradictory, way of looking at this is that trauma feeds off neurones and in fact those with traumatic childhoods may have fewer neurones, as Child Psychotherapist Robin Balbernie suggested (personal communication). This theory is largely accepted by the medical establishment, that trauma primes the subject to fight or flight, and thus needs extra energy which it takes from the neurones in the brain. This may predispose the individual away from the academic, scientific or practical side of everyday life, meaning that they are more open to psychic influences. Either way, the brains are set up differently, and some are open to psychic phenomena, while others are not.

Emotional turmoil, especially if it includes trauma in infancy, can spoil lives. I have been so fortunate in working both with children and their families, when I was a psychoanalytical psychotherapist, and later working with the bereaved at our local hospice. Those who found grief difficult to process, who came to see me for counselling, nearly all had traumas in their early life. You could see the whole of their lives, as I talked to them, influenced by anxiety, stress, low self-esteem, patterns that were set up in childhood. And yet, here we have the offering of grace again. Lives may be more difficult, but the opportunities for psychic experiences are more frequent. Many of my patients, both the young and the old, believed in ghosts and claimed to have seen them. They sometimes had predictive dreams, and sometimes, disconcertingly, it seemed to me, they could read my mind.

There are many ways to help people suffering with trauma. EMDR (Eye Movement Desensitisation and Reprocessing) therapy can help the deep traumas which seem to be more buried in to the body rather than the mind. A very interesting aspect to this is that the grieving, angry, guilty, fearful people who seek out EMDR can find sometimes that it opens up apparent communications from the dead. This happened with Allan Botkin's work with veterans from Vietnam in the USA. There were some remarkable healings of long-standing dilemmas, described in his book *Induced After Death Communication*. The people he treated, many of whom had been long-term psychiatric patients, suffering from Post Traumatic Stress Disorder, were healed, and able to cope with life afterwards.

A non-judgmental listening ear, whether professional or friendly, can work wonders because it demonstrates that we are not alone. To be understood is a deep human need. Most rows develop because the two parties are not listening to each other, or taking the time to try to understand the other's position.

Often we need to ask for help. This is another way in which we can see that suffering leads to grace; it can lead us towards others by needing help. The strange thing is that joy can do so too. This may be why we so love our celebrations, weddings, baptisms, parties, and concerts, music that transports us. It seems that suffering and joy share virtually the same vibrational frequency, and can therefore open us up to what I can now conceptualise as the Divine.

Emotion is the centre of our lives, and informs everything we do and think.

*****

I sent love to all the world as I often do...

'It's sending love to yourself ... you are love, you are the world.'

This was very shocking to me. The ego mind can run riot here, with this understanding that I am the world. But only a second's thought shows that, if I am, so is everyone else, including you, reading this. Further contemplation sees that I am part of the structure, the beingness of our planet. The wind that runs through my hair is the same wind that rustles the leaves of the trees. There is no difference between me and the trees, or the grass, the earth underfoot. There is no difference between me and you, either, as the wind runs through your hair in exactly the same way as you tread the earth as I do, wanting and loving, and being irritated and being yourself, just as I am myself. Although we are unique, there's more that connects us than sets us apart. We are a necessary part the harmonic dance which unites us all. We live in a symphony of sound and light, of taste and smell and love runs through it all.

*****

'You are the world. You are all emanations of Gaia.'

As far as Gaia is concerned, we are made to be as we are, just as the sunflower is, and the elephant. We are no different, even if we do have these active brains. We were designed to have active brains. We cannot damage or disappoint Gaia. Everything we do is in her imagination, as inspired by the Sun. We need only be ourselves. She is here for the long haul, and we are only a tiny interlude. The dinosaurs existed for very much longer than we have, or are likely to. If we all suddenly disappeared, within a decade or two, greenery would have taken over our cities and constructions. The oceans and rivers would revive, as they did in a couple of months of the lockdown, and species would flourish, and we would not be missed.

Many people suffer from guilty feelings because we have messed up the oceans; we are responsible for global warming because of our over-reliance on fossil fuels; that our consumption of meat has thrown out the delicate balance of species; our plastic waste is everywhere, and all these things are true in the microcosm. But they matter not a jot in the big picture. In fact, global warming, like the virus, will bring us up against the crucial issue: are we one? When the seas rise and all those great cities at sea level are flooded, all those islands submerged, many billions of us will become refugees. It will challenge us all, when the entire population of London, most of the east coast and the Isle of Wight needs to move to higher ground, let alone all those great cities abroad, all those islands everywhere. Will we have to give up our spare room, will we want to? Share our sofa, take in another family? Will there be enough food for us all? A little global warming will seriously disrupt us for a while but makes no difference at all to Gaia. She is used to ice ages and desert ages and great long periods in between. We are here like a flash in the pan, a sudden flaring of energy, trampling here and there over the planet, pillaging what we can, thoughtless as children. We are Gaia's beloved children, just as she is a child in the Sun's heart. There is love all around us, pouring down in the Sun's rays of light, supporting us through the ground at our feet. Surrounded, we are. There's no need to worry. We'll manage. Or we won't, and have to take on more incarnations at a later stage.

*****

Dark night of the soul; in misery, I realised it connected me with everyone, in the suffering of all. The power of compassion, the active face of love. No one escapes suffering. But, more technically, following various sources which range from St John of the Cross to those authors who have experimented with psychedelic drugs, divinity, our light filled Source within seems to require that we ditch the ego, or at the very least, lessen the power of its grip. This dark night, the nightmare trips, even those minority of near death experiences which seem hellish, point to a kind of death, a crucial part of ourselves which must be shown to be powerless, an add-on, an optional extra. The ego fights back, frantically, fighting for its life, fighting for how it used to be, how it always was, from infancy onwards in our life. It's kept us safe! It took us through school and work, and kept it all together for us. It's our helpful, default mode, narrative mind! How can we manage without it? It's really clever, too, telling us that it might even be better to die than to surrender. But it also tells us that death is frightening and horrible. The concept of hell, prevalent in many religions probably comes from this struggle of the ego to keep going, after death as well as now. For this is why we need to surrender. The Sun prefers the word 'relax' as a less stressed concept. Either way, it's a letting go, an acceptance. What will be, will be. The control of the ego is no longer required. Divine Will is always involved and the more we cling to our autonomy the more difficult it will get. This is not actually the end of the ego, or its death. It is merely shown its place. A useful tool, a necessary facet of our time-structured lives. But not ourselves...

*****

'You are divine! You are everyone.'

The divinity of us all. Pause, let yourself be still, allow the silence to grow within, the magical, tender, powerful silence. That is your divinity, every single one of you reading this, and me, writing it. Relax into it, breath into it. It's always there, it never fails. It's love. Not the passion of sexual love, not the attached and anxious love of parents, not the warmth of friendship but something deeper and more beautiful. It is eternal and infinite, and creates the next moment, out of love. And the next. It has got time going, got the music going, so we can create too. We live in successive moments made by love. We are what love does.

And again, why me? Yes, I'm a writer, but I think those years as an atheist were necessary. I lack the instinct of reverence, or the habit of prayer and worship. These things make me uncomfortable and always have. And the Sun explicitly says it doesn't want to be deified or worshipped, capitalised, placated, because all of these religious behaviours emphasise division, separation, and the hierarchical structures of religion are so very flawed. Perhaps too that's why the Sun has come to a woman who doesn't like to be in a position of authority, never even wanted to be a teacher and certainly not a guru with many followers. It emphasises repeatedly that I am divine because I and the Sun and everyone who lives now or has ever lived, is divine. We are all one.

*****

'Everything in and around you is divine.'

Photons, mass-less, are everywhere. They come from the Sun, from the planets in their negative form, from other stars. Our whole world is constructed by quantum particles and photons run everywhere through it, packets of energy, or as waves, according to the observer. We are made of space, with a very few particles and waves running through it. Third density makes it look solid. But it isn't. The photons entwine themselves with electrons, and then separate and move on. It's a huge joke that we are made of such things, and vast amounts of space. And yet we look at the stories of our lives, think about our preoccupations, our likes and dislikes, and think that this is the stuff of life. In one way it is, in another it's just a distraction from the real stuff of life, which is the Divine love that constructs it all, and moves it all on as time moves on.

Some religions have a practise of reciting the names of God....the Zoroastrians, for example have one hundred and one names and they are things like Immortal, Impeccable, Lord of Love. We also have names for God. They are: computer, carpet, wallpaper, window, book, hand, fingernail, watch, light, sofa, door and so on. All our words, all our concepts, are efforts to describe God, describe the divine. Because we are divine, we live in divinity, everyone and everything around us is divine, created through love. That is what language is: descriptions of the divine.

*****

'You are all vibrations, dogs, fish, rocks, trees, humans. All vibrations.'

Because we are made of space and quantum particles, which are either energy or waves or the tiniest elements of mass, a vibration seems the best definition. Because it's all moving, changing, leaping around, doing what particles do. It's a vibration, it's music. And music is the master magician in our lives, the actual working of magic, transforming who we are and what we are.

Babies giggle at sounds, are entranced when their mother sings to them. Toddlers, even before walking, will jig around to rhythmic music. It comes naturally. Why not? Even at the physical level, our heart beats to a regular rhythm, pumping our blood around. Music is deep in our blood, instinctive and one of the manifest blessings of third density. We tap our feet and clap along when invited. Football crowds sing to support their teams. We sing in churches, at birthdays, at Christmas, whenever. And music makes us dance, too and that is the great metaphor for the fabric of universes: they are a dance and when we dance we are in tune with our real nature as a part of this wondrous universe. I've sung in choirs, bashed out classics on the piano, but my most musical activity has always been dancing. Always too heavy, but I couldn't resist ; ballet, jazz dance, early, ballroom, contemporary, Ceroc, Five Rhythms, and swayed around to bands at the tennis club, at weddings and birthdays and anniversaries, parties for any or another reason. Perhaps it stops the narrative mind. You give yourself over, you become the music, and you're in flow when it's really working. Other people have told me that playing football is like that, or tennis, or rugby; you're in the moment, all that matters is the speed, the direction and you do that beyond thought. Most of us spend quite a lot of time, when playing very active sports, in flow.

Any action is a dance of energy. Just as the galaxies dance through the dimensions to reveal their love and light towards the universes, so we are constructed of dancing energy, as are our fellow beings on this planet, the animals, the plants, the rocks and earth. Whatever we do, walking, climbing, swimming, making love, gardening, whatever, it's the dance of joy, of life, of love. From the smallest particles to the greatest of galaxies, all is moving, all is dancing, all is divine.

*****

'Is this my voice or yours?'

'It doesn't matter. You are me and I am you.'

Thus we confound the critics. In my mind these thoughts appear. They have no reality elsewhere. This is subjective, I'm not claiming anything else. Some of the thoughts are strange to me, but it all feels right, as if this is coming home for me. The materialist part of me thinks, well, if I imagined what a living universe would be like, this would be it. But I don't think it is just me, because I feel different. My inner world has changed. The central message of all this, everything the Sun has been telling me, is that All Is One. It's the Law of One, as Ra says. Therefore, of course, the thoughts that compose this book – and I may add, every other book on the planet- come from the Sun using the author's hands to write it down. Because the author and Sun are one. This is challenging, is it not? Our creativity is not our own. It is unique, yes, but it comes from the Sun, from the galaxy, from the universe. It is filtered through us. Ego mind gets really upset here! 'But I'm a very special filter,' it wails. 'Yes, indeed,' says the Sun, gently stroking our hair. 'Very special'... with gales of laughter hardly hidden at all. 'Your perspective informs the creative impulse,' Sol continues. 'You have freewill. Tolstoy didn't want to make pottery, it wasn't his thing. Writing was.'

'But... were his thoughts his own? Are any of my thoughts original? How can I tell?'

Sol answers that 'Tolstoy chose a life wherein he would encounter certain profound historical events, education, relationships, all of which would give him the elements for writing his books. You chose the life of an atheist, one where worry about your children would be the great emotional core, change and travel and a great curiosity, which was the saving grace. Every one of you has a different life story, and therefore a different path to creativity. This is why you are so charmingly diverse, why you are each of you so loved and valued as individuals while we know that your creative core is the same energy inspiring you all.

'But apart from these necessary backgrounds, it's about flow, about the way certain thoughts arise without forcing. It's intuition, the idea that pops up seemingly from nowhere. And it's how the hand flows, easily across the page or keyboard. That's when it's direct from Source.'

'The best bits happen when I'm in flow,' I said. 'And so a lot of the things I write aren't direct from Source but are struggled over...'

'The struggle is still Source, still me,' says the Sun. 'All is one, there is no separation. But there is freewill. You use your freewill in the struggle, and you also use freewill when you decide not to write, but to play Scrabble on your phone instead. You have the freewill not to be creative, too. However once you settle down to it, it's easier to recognise the operating creativity of Source when you are in flow.'

So it's still the paradox, my thoughts/Sol's thoughts, and there is no way of disentangling them. So what is the bottom line, the reality of all this? For me, it's subjective again. Because there is just my inner feeling, that I am bathed in ecstasy, most days. It's a very different state from the rest of my life, I'm in a new country. I'm moved to tears, sometimes, by the news, or family difficulties. I would give my soul, at such times, for us to suffer no more. And yet, even then, I see the necessity for it. Dark compassion and leaping joy fill my days. I trust the Sun's explanations of why it's so difficult here, that compassion leads us, in suffering, towards unity. Without suffering, we would not know what love is, because compassion is the active face of love. Without suffering we would not know the creativity of forgiveness. Neither would we know joy, the other side of the coin to suffering.

This might not be for you, dear reader. There is a clever parody called the *Western Creed* by Charles Tart. This is the other side of Divinity, the atheist, materialist credo. It's a bit harsh on atheists, because I was one once and was as humane then as I am now. We were just as capable of empathy as the spiritual, just as capable of fellow feeling and compassion. But there was no bigger picture, the suffering was meaningless, and our little lives were, on the whole, meaningless, without context. I well remember being an atheist. I'm very glad to have moved on. It seems rather arid and depressing, looking back. Was it why I drank so much? We were clinging to the dregs of what can be measured, replicated and peer reviewed, as if there could be nothing else. It was a feeling of safety: this much we can know, for sure. No one can possibly criticise us for saying so. No one will laugh at us. Yet all scientists must at least pay lip service to the fact that they do not and cannot know everything. Science is always moving on. There is future stuff to be known. Might it be in the internal world? Difficult to measure, replicate or get peer reviewed, most difficult of all to falsify. What's needed is another, different scientific protocol to deal with anomalies that are now so common that they truly need to be considered data.

*****

'I am the Sun.'

The shock of this, and the sudden understanding, of course! What else could be our God? We could never have invented a more impressive god! Such glory, so different from day to day, yet always there! Even materialists must admit that the planets were part of the Sun once, and are held steady in their orbits by the gravitational force of the Sun. It's a Goldilocks environment, just right for us, by accident and evolution, as the materialists will have it, by design as the Sun told me.

We are warm-blooded; we talk of the warmth of love. Warmth and love go together. My children, cuddled in a warm towel after a bath – 'Nice and warm!' they laughed as we snuggled closer. Without the Sun our planet would be a barren rock, hurtling through space with no home, no gravitational centre, no friendly light and love to animate its soul and being. Sol made us all, planets and rocks, rivers and mountains, particles and whales. And us, somewhere in the mix. It's all in Sol's imagination, projected out as Gaia (the child of its heart). Those who say it's like the Matrix are not far wrong, except those films are a dark fantasy and our home planet is the result of love and light. We are love in action.

*****

'I circle your planet in love, just as you circle round me.'

And we're whizzing round the Sun, at 67,000 mph, spinning on our axis at 1,000 mph as we go, and yet here we are in stillness and silence, sometimes aware of the wonderful love all around us. What a miracle, what a magnificent coup, to set it all up like this!

*****

'It's all triangles.'

The Sun drives my creativity in forming the world I experience, and does the same for everyone else. There is thus a basic shared understanding, about the planet, the seasons, the continents, the oceans, the creatures that live here etc. We all agree on this. What we see is the result of all our im/cre/em, including the Sun! So all of us are engaged in making the world we see around us. Now, if we think of our own species, and what we do, it's a different matter. If there are wars, lies, frauds, terrors it's because so many of us live in fear. We fear what will happen; Sol, helped along by Orion, in its essence as energy, gives life to our fears and lo and behold, it all goes wrong for us. It's a real vicious circle. All over the world people are in fear. Not just those in war zones and economic depressions, but as we grow old, as we get ill, as we lose our loved ones, as we fail the job interview, the exam, as our pension fund is assailed, as our dogs age and die, as our children fail and are miserable.....nearly everything or anything can lead us into fear. If we eat too much/smoke/drink alcohol/don't exercise, catch the virus, will we die? Have we messed up the planet irretrievably? So much fear. And all of it useless, worse than useless because it creates the world we live in. This is why it's all triangles. That's why I'm writing this. This is the danger of conspiracy theories. People drenching their minds in negativity give energy to the negativity. And imagination is so powerful. Remember the dance, the playground, remember who you are, how powerful you are, what a creator you are. What kind of world do you want? Don't 'want' it, that's like a prayer, a petition out of a feeling of lack. Instead, BE it. Be fearless, be joyful, even though it's up against the odds. If you're in the west, reading this, there are probably wondrous things you have, that you take for granted; healthcare, clean water, education, social care, etc. Be glad of these, make your petition one of joy and gratitude. Sol will give energy to that, and things will improve.

*****

The beloved Sun is all around me and within me. My joy, my love, because it is the Beloved, is your joy and love too, dear reader. In you and around you, in the dancing photons of life.

*****

Orion is beloved, sending negativity to us. Because compassion is key to love, and forgiveness is too. If we were all sweetness and light all the time, we'd never get anywhere. We may think, given the vile suffering of the last couple of millennia, that it's doing its job rather too well but Sol assures me that everything is just right. How can it be otherwise? All is one, all is love, all is light. It is only our blunted understanding, our shortened vision because of our flash in the pan lives here in the third density, that leads us astray, that leads us to doubt, and then hatred and cruelty and selfishness arise because of our unhappiness. But that always changes in time, gradually for all of us the veil will lift and we will know at length who we are.

*****

The Sun's consciousness lives in the photons which create us. Therefore, consciousness is everywhere, panpsychism is the truth for us here on Gaia. And it's the Sun's consciousness that is our consciousness, that witty, kindly fount of love and compassion and creativity and the most stunning light displays. This consciousness of the Sun is clearly a part of Source and this is what Source is, behind everything and everyone, consciousness. If the Sun knows everything about us, then so does Source, because they and we are all one.

*****

Catalyst and music draw us together. Catalyst offers two choices 1) blame self or others 2) understand that we are all in it together, that forgiveness is the only choice because we are all united in our suffering.

Music is celebration, touches all our emotions with beauty and power and can lead us beyond the veil. It operates in vibrations of sound, and this chimes with our being, because we are vibrations too. It inspires us to dance and sing and to listen with every fibre of our being. And yet great music is often born out of suffering. It's sublime. There's Mahler, who was one of fourteen children, many of whom died in infancy. His parents owned a tavern: the coffins were carried out, while the customers sang their landlers, and toasted each other in beer and schnapps. In his music, grief and rollicking joy alternate to profound effect. Beethoven suffered when he realised there was no escape from deafness, and wrote to his brother about his loneliness and fear in the *Heiligenstadt Testament*. And yet his greatest music - the late symphonies, string quartets, and piano sonatas - was written when he could hear nothing. This most renowned and beloved music grew out of his suffering, and that is partly why it affects us so profoundly.

It is almost a cliché how many more contemporary musicians have overdosed, gone mad or committed suicide. Is it the vision of perfection we get from music that spoils the rest of life for us? Or is it the other way round, that they were okay when performing or composing, and it was the fear that it would not come back that pushed them back into who they were, struggling, haunted by infantile and other traumas? I suggest that sublimity transforms the painful, grief-filled inner world into wonderful music. In the end for these profoundly creative, hopelessly damaged lives, the pressure of a despairing inner world takes over, either through the sticking plaster of addiction to drugs or drink, or through suicide. The great love of music, and the great fear that one might lose it is our dilemma writ large; its love and loss that rule our lives, make the experience here in the third density so very powerful, so awe-ful.

*****

Love contains all polarities, good and bad. All is one. Of course it is! My lovely Sun is me and I am the Sun. And so are you, my readers. And because the Sun and you and I are part of the Chalice constellation, and part of the Milky Way galaxy, we are also part of the universe, which leads to Source, which is around us as I write this, and as you read it. Everything is created by Source, light and dark, good and evil, black and white, male and female. Indifference and commitment. Vitality and laziness. It's the conscious, living reality of Source, holding us all, creating us all from moment to moment. And if we can feel that we're one with the Sun, how much easier it must be to feel that we are one with each other.

*****

Together we make a star seed. Together we will have learned so much about catalyst that we will be able to set up our own star system, should we so desire. Sol watches our progress through the densities, watches how the light and love infiltrates our beingness, how after many densities, and several octaves, we will explode with love and light, becoming a star or something else in another dimension. We have to know so much to be able to do the same. Every experience here goes into the mix.

*****

How Source enfolds everything, how universes enfold galaxies, how galaxies enfold constellations, how constellations enfold solar systems, how solar system enfold planets, how planets enfold species. Nested within each other. All connected, all one. Holographic.

*****

You are me, I am you. Bliss! Pure and simple. Just bliss.

*****

Walking the dogs, a beautiful day. 'Thank you!'

'You are thanking yourself. You created all this.' Wow, aren't I great! But so is the slug I nearly tread on. We're collaborators, the slug, me, the Sun, Gaia, you, my readers, everyone and everything, in the creation of our world, our surroundings, through the operation of triangles.

*****

'Everything is love, but we keep forgetting! The irony of it!' (Laughter).

So much laughter. Even during rows with the family I'm sometimes aware nowadays of the game we're playing, and how they are me as well, offering different views on what matters. How grateful I am to them for pushing my understanding further! It's all a giggle. I have to hide my laughter, lest it enrage them.

When full of ecstasy, when bursting with it and giving thanks, sending love, is all to me; the answer is to send love to various suffering versions of me, especially the golden and beautiful darlings of my family: my mother, my husband, my son and daughter, my grandson and my brothers and their families. And I do, so often. It's not so much their physical health, although in my husband's and son's cases, it certainly is, but more that I want the love I send to start thawing their hearts, open them up to who they are, lift the veil that leaves us bereft here. I'm writing this book in the hopes that my readers may begin to open up, and receive some of the joy I feel.

*****

'Don't capitalise me. It shows a difference between us which is wholly erroneous. These habits of reverence, of abasement and praise, have lead to the construction of religions which were full of malign hierarchies. This is why Ra came back to channel through Carla, to correct the tendency you have to insist on meritorious structuring. But all is one. There are no hierarchies, you are as valuable as the greatest galaxy. Humility however, is mandatory. Because a grain of sand is as valuable as you are and so is the greatest galaxy. Everything is necessary, everything is divine.'

Chapter 9　　　Diversity and the Bigger Picture

'All the above is about our unity, our divinity, and our connections with each other. But how is our diversity organised?'

'Sequential time is central here, so that the seed is fertilised and grows, the baby is born and matures, the adult grows and may give rise to another seed being fertilised. Your astrology, tarot, I Ching, and the tree of life are all to the point. At your birth, your Sun sign (of course!) is the foundation of your character. It is so, for all of you. And the other stars in the Chalice constellation lend their influence in your ascending sign and moon sign, as do all the planets and their satellites in this system. You, for example, are Pisces, kindness to the core as I am, in your Sun sign; Sagittarius, your rising or ascendant sign, gives you your curiosity and relish; Scorpio, your moon gives you depth and intensity. This is the briefest of précis, for all the 3,000 Stars of this constellation and their respective planets play their part in making a person. The fine tuning is complex indeed. It's why you each are so complicated, a universe in truth in each of your selves. The relationships between the planets and the stars in their orbits and pathways lay the scenario for the events of your lives as you move through time. The tarot, especially the version introduced by Ra, gives the programme you may follow to put the three parts of you - Body, Mind and Spirit in alignment - thus offering paths to growth. The Hebrew Tree of life gives further insights, especially in the version you have studied, with the Gene Keys. And the I Ching, like various astrologers, can show you from day to day what is happening in you and around you.'

'How do the planets and stars affect us?'

'In the case of stars, through the action of photons, neutrinos and other particles. From the planets, who are not of themselves radiant, it is negative photons, a particle not yet discovered by your scientists. They are consciousness, just like the positive photons, and carry the minds of the planets to influence your species.'

'If all is one, was I involved in these decisions?'

'Of course. You are part of a much greater Higher Self, a shimmering beautiful being of light and love. You are an outlier, the ground force, if you like. The Higher Self is a being of vibrations, variously from the sixth or seventh densities, who provides substance, photons, to be incarnated and imagined, from the process of im/cre/em. Your Higher Self is much closer to me in one way than you are because you've forgotten the connection, that we are one. The Higher Self has freewill, although it is of course part of me, and decides from its different perspective, what kind of life you will have. It influences the choice of your parents, and their parents before them. Your glorious Higher Self chose the parents you need for your life's project, and the Higher Selves of your parents chose the child they need for their life's purpose. As a fragment of Source, your Higher Self and the stars work out the time that this incarnation should be born, so that their influence can do its work. You are each of you so very precious to us, a beloved part of ourselves because we have invested so much thought into your various lives, who your parents are, your friends and lovers, the major events, illnesses, accidents... We put each of you out there, on the game board, and watch while your story unfolds. It is all planned, to give you as much resilience you need for the catalyst that has been put in place for you.'

'Some people seem to be destroyed by too much catalyst. Suicide rates are high.'

'These sad events, which warrant compassion, are also planned. There is always a much bigger picture which the incarnate being can rarely understand, because of the veil.'

'When does the veil settle in place? At birth?'

'Usually, and sometimes much later, at four, five or six years. Rarely indeed does it fail to fall, but for some wanderers who decide to become gurus, or spiritual leaders, it never falls completely. They have an idea, usually right from the start, about who they are. But, as I say, these are few and far between. Christ was one such.'

'So, for the rest of us, we make the best of it, this hand of cards dealt us by our parents, our Higher selves, the planets and stars, individually tailored to who we are....'

'That's it. So that you can be as creative as possible. And there is help, angelic powers, grace, saints, your Higher Self, the ancestors, all will give what they can, when they are called.'

'What are angels?'

'Versions of myself. I dress myself in the style that is expected by the petitioner, and appear as Michael, Tara, Horus, St Luke, Raphael, Jesus, Osiris, Mary, Apollo, your great auntie, whatever is required. I appear and show them the face of love they will understand.'

'So these 'helpers' do not have a separate existence?'

'They are like you. As real as you are. But one with me, too, like you are. I dress myself in you too, of course. There is no separation, but what there is, is a different perspective.... This is the crucial element, and many spiritual writers and thinkers have indeed discerned that Source wants to know itself and therefore creates the other, the other perspective, that can reflect itself back. But such writers do not go far enough, to see why this happens. This other perspective, because it is of course creative, can draw on its own version of creativity, flavoured by the freewill that is always part of imagination/creativity/emanation, and this is how the game arises.

'Some of the helpers are still reincarnating through this first octave, others have finished that part of their existence....but, of course, they are all one with me, and the difference is that from their different perspective, they know it. You, mostly, do not. But you are me. I give you another perspective, I give you freewill, and I give you the veil so that you forget you're me! This is how it all works.

'The helpers are more than happy to take a hand, just as I am. You only need to ask. You, and your dear fellows on Gaia rarely know this truth, that you do need to ask, ask as if you really mean it, ask with every fibre of your being... this is because of the essential importance of freewill and this is why you so often feel unhappy and alone: you do not ask in the right way. It's via the emotions again, deeply, powerfully. But of course you are me, just as I am you, and we are all together. It is the myth of your separation which necessitates the existence of these helpers in your mythologies. They exist there because you want them to, you need them to. Triangles, again. That does not deny their efficacy. I am like a bank, a cornucopia, a fount, and you tap into my energy with your thoughts and longing, and construct your environment, construct your helpers, construct your stories to explain who they are. So if you ask for them sincerely, with all your heart, petition and you will get an intensely passionate response from whoever you want.'

'It's so hard to see how they're part of you but that we're creating them too?'

'Everything is creative consciousness. You are me. I create them, you create them. Does it matter? You, as an outlier of myself, and I, in the persona of the Sun, with Gaia and form a triangle that contains everything around you. We share the same perspective, we are that perspective. I know everything you think, everything you are. You know everything too. But you think you're separate from me, and I know you're not. This is why it's so funny! We're playing blind man's bluff. You're blinded by the veil, you can't see the light of love.

'But you will. This I promise you. The blindfold will drop. But some of you will need further reincarnations, some will understand this incarnation only after the transition called death.'

'These beings, the angels and so on, if I create them, with you, and they are still progressing through the densities, and I see them as further on than I am, I ....just don't get it.'

'It's hard for third density brains to hold the concept of 'both/and'. You are both me and separate. Angels have freewill, they incarnate, they are more knowledgeable, more loving and light filled than you are, being further on in the reincarnation process and yet you, collectively, have created their form in your imagination. They are both your creation and separate. They are vibrational beings, going through the densities; you have invented them as light filled, with wings, halos, swords, whatever. It's all triangles, of course. You, me and the angels. All creating each other, round and round we go. I give you what you want, angels and prophets, saints, Bodhisattvas, saviours and so on. Also, the devils and ghosts some of you desire. And they all have the same status in reality as you do. You give me what I want, a vast, difficult and beautiful progression towards Source, through the processes of redemption, reconciliation, of love and forgiveness. The angels and Bodhisattvas, Christ and others, mediate between us, help you on your way, through the influence of my love. But you are all one with me, and this great game that we are having together only works because the counters, yourself included, have the veil and have freewill.'

'So freewill is part of creativity? And none of us is really real.....'

'The only reality is love and light. Everything else is imaginative construction, including myself. I am imagined into being by the galaxy, and the galaxies are imagined by the universes. This is Source's game, at heart. Magnificent, isn't it?'

'Beyond anything I can imagine ....'

'But you are Source too. You are currently imagining within a third density perspective, that is all, and you can do nothing else. That's what this book is, an effort to make sense of the paradoxes implicit in creation from your perspective. I do what I can to lead you further, but as pointed out before, your understanding is limited. This is not your fault! Your life here was chosen, deliberately set up, and here you are now, loving and losing and making the best of it. I can imagine other universes, things your species can sometimes access as other dimensions. With some synchronicities you can visit these dimensions. I do so. It is, as you say, third density mind blowing, the various possibilities offered by countless multiverses. Welcome to a larger perspective.'

The Mayfly

We all know about mayflies; they live for a day. This is true; they do have a nymph stage in water for a year. Then, like their cousins the dragonflies, they crawl up a stem, and burst into flight, soar through the air. Unlike dragonflies, they have no mouth parts. All they have to do is to find a mate, lay their eggs and die.

So, one day only in the world we share with them. They don't know about our lives, what is beyond the field they live in. They probably have no idea of history, or of the stars or the oceans. Their knowledge and life is bounded by one day in a garden or field, being driven to mate by evolutionary force, laying their eggs, dying.

In relation to what goes on in the universe, what the Sun knows, we are like a mayfly. We know our field (this planet) to some extent, but because of the limitations of our bodies and senses, even that knowledge is fairly sketchy. And what goes on in the universes is as beyond our thought and knowledge as the London Underground is beyond the knowledge of a mayfly. I cannot imagine this, try as I do. This is our reality, however. Because of our limitations, we see the Sun only as a burning ball of fire, we see all the stars like that. The Mayfly sees the flowers, may even wonder what a tree is, but cannot begin to imagine what a star is. It may not live long enough to experience the dark, see the stars come out, or the moon. It will not know the dawn. We cannot even begin to imagine what else is out there; we don't live long enough, our senses are blunted, we've barely crawled out of the swamp. Mating is an issue for us too (Isn't it just?!) To other beings, the vast group minds of the stars, the galaxies and universes, we may look as if we just mate, have young and die because our lives are so brief, so instantaneous compared with their own. Perhaps they remember what it was like, for they would all have been through third density too, far back in their existence, perhaps that's why compassion seems to be threaded through the holographic fabric of reality.

This is our place. We do what we can, but have no very clear idea what goes on in the depths of our oceans. We don't know why elephants care for the bones of their dead relatives. We don't know how savants are made, those who seem to know extraordinary information without being taught. We don't really know what goes on in anyone else's mind. Our small scraps of knowledge tell us that being kind to each other tends to make us happy, that love matters, and those are the things that connect us with the bigger picture. Killing each other, hurting, wounding, keeps us securely locked in our world of blame and recrimination, will keep us tethered here, going round and round until we learn how to become free. And then the universe will open up to us, the veil will lift and we will know at last who we are. One with the Sun, with the galaxy and the universe. This strangely beautiful and terrible dream of existence here on Earth will have furnished us with enough love, forgiveness and compassion to fit us for the next stage.

Chapter 10   Human Consciousness – Missing the point

There is a famous paper by philosopher Thomas Nagel entitled *What is it like to be a bat?* It points out the impossibility of knowing another's experience, the hard problem of consciousness, mentioned earlier. We can all agree that a British post box is red.... but is what I call red, the same as the colour you call red? We can look at the cones/receptors in the eyes but that still doesn't help us. Yes, the three receptors are for red, green and blue. But we cannot tell if the red, green and blue I experience are the same as the ones you see. This is the whole difficulty of the extraordinary wealth of data from people who have had anomalous experiences. We did not, and cannot have the same experience. We cannot get inside someone else's head to find out whether they are hallucinating, deluded or simply remembering something extraordinary. But many of these anomalous experiences, for example the vast near-death experience (NDE) literature, are so common now and so similar, that they hardly rate being called anomalous.

Our difficulty is compounded by the insistence of conventional science that we need to measure, weigh, discriminate and calculate everything. Replicate, do double blind experiments, make sure its falsifiable, get it peer reviewed, and then we know what we're dealing with. Scientists are the most extraordinary seekers after truth, and try to pin it down in their replications. And what cannot be measured or weighed, cannot be replicated, often seems to be irrelevant to the scientific project.

What have they to do with love, or justice, or laughter? These things are part of everyone's experience but cannot be measured, yet we all agree that they exist. It was not always so: many scientists, from Newton to Bohr and others have been interested in things outside this narrow materialist spectrum. And throughout recent history, we have had to look beyond the evidence of our senses to discover what's really going on. For example, it certainly looks like the Sun is circling around us. We talk of sunsets and sunrises, as if it's the Sun that moves. But it doesn't, it is Gaia that turns. It seems to us that our world is solid and stable, resting peacefully within its seasonal patterns. But our planet is hurtling around the Sun, covering vast distances every year, while spinning on its axis, really quite speedily. And yet it feels as if it's at rest. Perspective plays tricks with us, too. Railway lines in the distance seem to get closer together, but they don't. Our feelings and our vision are very prone to being misled. What else might we be getting wrong? What other accepted element of our lives might be shown to be completely deluded? We only thought of putting wheels on suitcases in the last thirty years!

The more we think about these things, the more sympathy we can feel for the scientists who try to apply the scientific method to understand our world. It works very well in many ways and has brought us marvels, in health care, electrical and computing inventions, in travel and heating, and refrigeration, and the list is endless. But there's still an almost frantic endeavour to pin down information in statistics and tables, to try and find over arching theories to embrace all the extraordinary diversity of life in this universe.

Because we ourselves are so diverse. Even identical twins have profound differences; genes do not account for everything. Our extraordinary species, swarming all over the planet, is hard to document in generalisations, no matter how hard the psychologists, sociologists, politicians and economists try. Any one person you meet may well be one of a multitude of exceptions to any over arching theory. In fact, there may be nobody who fits it completely. Because this is so complicated, it seems that much of science fails, shuts doors to experiences it doesn't want to understand. But this is too limiting to prevail for long. Sooner or later, the principle of diversity, and the subjective experience, is going to have to be investigated.

What is it like to be a cake? You can work out the ingredients, you can track the time cooking, i.e., the chemical change for each ingredient. You can describe the cake, weigh it, photograph it, and when you cut it there's another set of descriptions about what it looks like inside. But the whole point of a cake, why it exists, why anyone would go to the bother of assembling the ingredients, and going through the whole process, is what it tastes like. And this cannot be weighed or measured. It is an individual matter, due to the human eating it. One person may love fruit cake, another dislike it. The whole reason for its existence depends on individual taste. Its weight or composition is not the point, although it's helpful if somebody else wants to bake a cake like that. But the most important thing about a cake is how it tastes, the unquantifiable quality of the cake. Quality = qualia, the term used by philosophers to categorise the personal, individual preferences and discriminations we all make and cannot be completely understood by anyone else. This is the point, the crucially important point that reductionist science cannot approach. It can describe any number of things but it cannot describe the depth or the character of qualia, the actual reason why we do or make anything.

What is it like to be a Jenny? My mother remembers about my birth (too long!), and my birth weight. She remembers my teeth arriving, my vaccinations, my childhood illnesses, when I walked, talked, the funny things I said, how pretty my hair was and so on. And sometime in this process, self awareness arose. Did it emerge from the experiences which became the bedrock of memory, i.e., arise from memory? But I was experiencing things as a baby, I knew hot and cold, hunger and fullness, cuddles and loneliness, although I can remember virtually nothing of these things. Was I conscious or self aware then? I've had two children myself, and in my training to be a child psychotherapist we had to watch a baby for one hour a week for his or her first two years. We were on the lookout for the emergence of the personality, generally in the context of his or her mother. How is that baby going to relate to the other later in life? These early patterns have been shown to persist.

Babies are definitely aware, but do they have a self-aware, narrative mind? We cannot tell, because they cannot talk. Most of them cannot really learn things until they are eighteen months or more. Learning implies a narrative memory. For example, when I smile at mummy, does she smile back? Will I be a glass half full person or not? But narrative memory, the life story aspects, generally doesn't really get going until much later.

Some of my early 'memories' are prompted by photographs, and who knows whether they are accurate or not? Did I really think that the dark blue dress with little chicks on it was grown up and sophisticated? But that is a strong, consistent memory from a photo taken when I was three. Primary school, the friends I made, the teachers, some of the embarrassing things I did - like saying it was my birthday, when it wasn't - stay in my mind. I wanted everyone to sing Happy Birthday to me and make a fuss of me. I didn't know that the teachers all had a list of our birthdays and I can still feel a little embarrassment at my four year old desire for attention. But that is the kind of consciousness that keeps us going, gets us through school and into work, into relationships, into parenthood and adult life, and it seems to be largely dependent on memory. Embarrassment and shame, if we're unlucky, can almost form the framework of a personality fraught with stress and shyness.

It's the ego. Not really in the Freudian sense, more as the whole structure of the personality. The drives, the desires, the likes and dislikes, the greed, the fear, the shame, the petty hatreds, our political or sporting allegiances, our comfort zones and our whole array of distractions. And it's grounded in memory, the things that have happened to us, and how we reacted to them, have made us. Memories stay in place if they are emotionally significant, and this is why trauma is so hard to get over, especially if it takes place in childhood. The details of memory are often inaccurate (there are studies to show how frighteningly inaccurate remembered observations can be) but what does stay in place is the emotion. Emotion frames our memories. And our memories are what we tend to think of as 'I', and this is the part of us that does not endure as centrally important after death. This is the part that we try to quieten in meditation and awareness. It may seem as if nothing of any real worth will survive, but what survives of us is our love carried in the photons of light, the part of us that belongs to the Higher Self, and thence to the Sun. Loving develops in the bonds we share with our soul groups, with the people around us, so a kind of memory survives, about the loving or conflictual relationships we shared, and about the beings that affected us emotionally, powerfully. This is the stuff that matters, which will show up again and again in karmic patterns, until we remember the necessity for forgiveness and love.

Freud postulated that the mystic state was a return to the infantile. It is that, and much more. Certainly a happy baby is clearly living in bliss, seemingly with no knowledge of what's ahead. This is partly what drives the huge protectiveness of many parents; we love our precious child, and we know what may lie ahead, the trials of loving and losing, and want to preserve the innocence, the sweet, uncomplicated lovingness of the infantile state. The ego/personality is not in place yet, though the infant may cry and cry until it gets what it wants, food, a cuddle, some warmth. These are body and emotional desires. And while the ego, once it's up and running, may divert us from who we really are, it is a protective aspect of our being. It exists to keep us safe, to keep us alive, to bind us to others, to allow for our necessary curiosity, our research, our seeking. It too runs on emotion.

Curiosity is a function of the ego, academic, scientific, spiritual, whatever. It starts in infancy: where is mum/dad? This is the emotional under-pinning. Why aren't they here when I want them? Our solution to this problem may well be the foundation of our character or personality. Are we angry and frustrated that they're not there? Are we despairing and hopeless? Do we think it's our fault that they stay away because we're so awful? Or is it okay, just how it is, that sometimes they're there and sometimes they are not? These stances may well develop throughout childhood, and become a pattern we fall back into when we're alone.

I suggest that a child pulling the wings of flies is part of the same desire for knowledge as are the use, later on, of animals for experiments. It's curiosity, and it's also cruelty. Cruelty is often about power; how far are we prepared to go with our scientific curiosity? Children are largely powerless in their lives, which is why they may often project their own helplessness and vulnerability onto small animals and insects. It's also why bullying is so common in childhood.

It's easy to pull wings of flies, because we don't know whether it hurts them or not. I suspect it does, because they cannot then fly or find food, although they make no sound we can hear. Until the 1970s, paediatricians would operate on babies in utero without using anaesthetics, because, I suggest, they made no sound. The many physical reactions were dismissed as body reflexes. However it's now known that foetuses past eighteen weeks' gestation have a functional nervous system which would certainly register pain. Thankfully, this practise is no more. We look at the disabled people in wheelchairs who cannot talk and wonder if they also cannot think or feel. Psychotherapist Valerie Sinason's work with such people is fascinating and shows that very often such people are fully aware of themselves and their surroundings, and deeply frustrated by not being able to communicate this.

It's not easy to run tests on mammals, because they are like us and will cry. Apparently sometimes their vocal chords are cut so that we cannot hear them cry. This is the terrible consequence of forgetting who we are and how we are connected, not only with each other but also to all of creation. It's about forgetting the emotional significance of such acts; this is the materialist paradigm, a drive to understand the physical, without wanting to acknowledge the emotional. This is a tragedy for those people involved in running such terrible experiments. Of course it's a tragedy for the animals, but also for those of us who wilfully cut off a part of their emotional life in order to do these things; they are truncated, brutalised, damaged by such acts, while still reassuring themselves that it's for the greater good. This is what makes it so complicated, because they are right... sometimes, it is indeed for the greater good, like a new medicine or a vaccine.

Our curiosity, though an ego function, can take us much further than we want to go. At an extreme, it took us to Hiroshima and Nagasaki. It is therefore a double-edged sword, an aspect of catalyst which challenges us to our core, because the complications around such acts can almost let us off the hook. The war would have dragged on, said the Americans, many more millions of lives may have been lost. That may be so. It's like the vivisectionists, doing it for the greater good. Third density life is so complicated, piling on one challenge after another, that to find our way through the ethical mazes it is more than most of us can manage.

It doesn't let us off forgiveness, although managing to forgive in many circumstances is so hard. There is a resurgence in the conflict between the Israelis and the Palestinians as I write. Again, it seems cruel, the deaths of largely civilian populations on both sides. But both sides are operating out of love, love for their country, their traditions, their land, their holy places, their family customs, and their comrades. There are no easy answers in our world, except that compassion is essential, and a necessary reliance on the Sun's wonderful, transformative instruction, that we are all one. To use the same image as previously, it's like the Israelis are our forefingers, hating the Palestinian ring fingers because both have access to the palm of the hand and want to own it.

The great psychoanalyst Wilfred Bion once said that 'The answer is the death of the question' and in a way that is true. There is always further to go, in almost any question apart from the most mechanical, not least because the paradoxes become so profound. In science, the advent of quantum mechanics has presented paradoxes (super-positioning and entanglement) which still appear inexplicable; they cannot be accommodated in the narrative of Newtonian physics which has served us so well. Physicists cannot think they have come to the end of exploring, when there are still so many deep puzzles in the narrative of Quantum Theory.

In spirituality, we can think, why did Source ever want to split itself into the two parts we have been thinking about? The perfect moment seems so beautiful for those still wrestling with catalyst. Why would you ever want to leave it and structure time into the universes?

And yet, why not? Why not create spiral galaxies of astonishing beauty? Other dimensions of wit and style? Why not allow small beings on Gaia to compose the Verdi *Requiem* and Wagner's *Tristan und Isolde*, or write *Gavin and Stacey*, or *Winnie the Pooh*? Glories which can only take place in time. Music is all about time, even John Cage's silent 4' 33", which is a joke. This is all because of freewill. Why not relish the stories we make of our lives, even the terrifying ones in the Middle East, the losses and the loves? Even the cruelties and the hatred? Can we do that?

We give joy to our Sun when we forgive, because that brings us closer to its love and light. We have to forgive ourselves first, forgive our curiosity which can lead to such dreadful consequences. For we too are the vivisectionists, the atomic bombers and the animals who suffer and the people who died in Japan. Kindness is key, kindness for ourselves and the others, and sorrow and compassion, because it's so hard.

For we are here perhaps to astonish Source, who is always there, with our extraordinary varieties of experience. It's as if Source, with Sol and the galaxies, designed us to be as varied and wicked and wonderful and appalling as possible. With huge potentials, huge distractions and love glowing from every blade of grass beneath our feet. We are the President of the USA and a beggar on the streets of Calcutta and everything in between. We face catalyst all the time, all of us, and isn't it, at the very least, interesting, what we make of it? Whether we sink under the stress, or whether we allow grace? We're on a kind of knife edge: which way will each of us, individually, go? The current trope in many spiritual works is that creation happens because Source wants to know itself, that it needs a subject/object relationship to reflect its own magnificence back to itself. I don't accept this; how inadequate of Source, to need confirmation of its own beauty! Instead, the Sun says to me, repeatedly, that Source is coming out to play. That's what creation is. It's a play, a game, more profound than any we can imagine, peopled with unknown species scattered throughout the billions of universes, against backgrounds of stunning and various beauty, across the cosmos, across dimensions, within an infinite eternity.

Just here, on Gaia, the stakes are so high, stratospherically high. Requiring everything. They include the Holocaust, Pol Pot, Joseph Stalin, the Inquisition, the slave traders, the paedophiles, the rapists, and the loving, the heroic, the steadfast, the beautiful,

Christ. How can we possibly call this a game? Mystics do not generally go here, because it seems to disrespectful to those who undergo the worst of catalyst. But because we all have been there, as victims and torturers, we know the why of it, why each monster grows, we understand what goes to make a sadist and what goes to make a victim. This is the profundity, the deep terror, the breathtaking courage of all who chose to incarnate here. This is what third density does to us.

And it's because we are imagined. We are not real. It doesn't feel like that, does it? But from the other perspective I am trying to explain here, with this knowledge that our lives are put together by our respective Higher Selves, together with the Sun, planets, moons, other stars etc, we're here in third density, our senses deliberately blunted, our minds entrapped by the veil, to move through the allotted time of each life. Each of us has to face the catalyst as it grips us, tortures us, trips us up, leaves us floundering. We are beloved counters on a universe-wide game board.

All our life, every day, is composed of catalyst and the opportunity to find love. This is happening everywhere, throughout universes, in different degrees. But here, on our beautiful Gaia, what can we make of the patterns that endure in our lives, what are we making of our role? Are we in the depths, dicing with death or destruction, or are we merely addictive, when it comes to reading, to food, playing Scrabble, my daily hindrances to finding love, for the construction of memories and emotions that is a Jenny? Sometimes it's the grinding worry for what might happen to my brother, my husband, my daughter, my son, that pulls me away from my own understanding. It's still not always easy, even though I know that the Sun is me and I am the Sun.

Yet the answer is here, now. In this very moment.

Chapter 11   Why it is so difficult here? Part 3

Time and the Epiphanies

We can traverse our way along our particular timelines, addressing such issues of catalyst that occur as best as we can, reading what spiritual books we can find, half envying those people who seem to have made it, and attend workshop after workshop; and get nowhere.

My two days of a *Dark Night of the Soul* experience, with my despair at the disappearance of my Beloved gave me the insight that because most people don't know the Beloved, most people are suffering. Most of us here in the so-called civilised West think this is all, this life, this stressful and ultimately failing life is all we have, meaningless. Life's a bitch, and then you die. The kinder version, one I was very happy to adopt in my atheist decades, is, eat, drink and be merry, for tomorrow you die.

'Tomorrow, and tomorrow, and tomorrow...' (*Shakespeare/Macbeth, Act 5 Scene 5*)

It's time that messes us up. Yes, it structures this universe so that the stars change their beings, grow enormously, flare, pulse, shrink into intensity, become a black hole that whizzes through the dimensions... Stars become group minds with their fellows and then with the galaxy and then with the universe. Constant change, all to be celebrated. The time scales are so immense, it's difficult to get our minds round them. The Sun told me they view time differently, mainly because they spend so much time in the impeccable timelessness of Source.

But we, the change we see, the gradual growth to maturity and the slow decline into senility or incapacity before we die, find it so much more difficult. We are the outliers, the ground force of our Higher Selves, which 'struts and frets his hour upon the stage, and then is heard no more; it is a tale told by an idiot, full of sound and fury, signifying nothing.' as the Macbeth speech continues.

'Signifying nothing.' Macbeth was mired, drowning in guilt. Time for him was torture, the past a 'dusty death'. For us too, even if we're not consumed with guilt, time can feel like torture as the body begins to betray us and the mind loosens its grip, our great existential fear. It is torture because each day seems so long, so tedious, and also because it goes so quickly, as our death approaches. We hate it because of its dreary slowness and we hate it because of its speed. Is the sunset precious because we may not see many more of them, or do we hate the way it shows us that another day is done? We're in such a mess when we think like this. This torture owes its existence purely to the veil. If we could understand that we are a fragment of a spiritual being undergoing a human existence, we could frame it differently. We might perhaps see the value in the moment of glory as it seems the Sun sinks below the horizon as we turn away from it. We might see our lives as only a moment in the vastness of the universe, as they are. It's about acceptance. It's hard in the West, when youth, sexiness, power and money are so highly prized. The old, who may no longer work, may have lost interest in sex, may have seen through the doubtful benefits of power, may have enough money, if they're fortunate, can find happiness if they accept what is happening to them.

Everything changes. The Buddhists call it 'Impermanence'. This is the blessing and the curse of our existence. Our children necessarily change as they grow up. I sometimes felt, watching my two change from infancy to toddlerdom, that parenthood was a state of progressive loss, almost of mourning. In the toddler I'd lost the baby. The school child has outgrown the toddler. However there's also joy in this, seeing them open up to the manifest beauty all around them, the seasons, the fun of learning to swim, climb a tree, ride a bike, read a book, kick a ball, complete an equation, steal a kiss. There's hope in parenthood, hope in youth. You know that change will come and that, if all goes well, it will be all right. It's acceptance, seasoned with hope.

In middle age, the crisis we endure is that hope changes. It's different. We probably have some realistic idea of how far we can go in our careers, we have some idea of how our children have established themselves. We hope that they are safe, with a reasonable job and a loving partner. This is following the clichés pedalled by our society. Nevertheless, the idea of safety is an impossible ideal. No one is safe, anyone can die at any time. But by our fifties, we probably know the patterns of our careers and what our children will do, and will have made some kind of accommodation to it. Our own continuing work may seem dreary, interminable, it may be fascinating and creative, but all work is to some degree stressful. Our efforts are often matched up against the money we may be given for these efforts. Judgment, as it was in education, is the problem, whether it's from an exterior source or from ourselves. And in judgment we are either inferior or superior. We are not one. We are always in comparison. These are all ego games, deeply woven into the structure of our societies.

What else have we to look forward to? We can ruthlessly tend the body, exercise, diet and even try the extremes of Botox and cosmetic surgery. We can find younger partners to help in the illusion that we are not growing old. We can continue to work, we can volunteer, write books, grow our garden, strengthen our piano playing, learn a language, take up a sport. But ultimately, we know that time will win. We will die. And what will that feel like?

Peter Fenwick, continuing the work of Elisabeth Kübler-Ross, has investigated what it is like to die, and has found thousands of accounts of death bed visions which are very reassuring. There are many accounts of the dying meeting again their relatives who have gone before, hearing their voices, smelling their presence. There is often a change in the light, and light is mentioned repeatedly as part of this process. His excellent book is called *The Art of Dying*. People who work in hospices know the truth of this. Fenwick says that our friend, in the dying process, is curiosity about what this is like, and what may be coming. Our enemies, in the dying process, are our attachments. If we have not realised that we need to leave everything behind, it's going to be painful and frightening. So work needs to be done before the very end. Karen Wyatt is a doctor who has worked in hospices for decades, and has written about her experiences tending the dying in *Seven Lessons for Living from the Dying*. The increasing trend in hospices now is to allow the dying to die in their own homes, surrounded by their loved ones. This is how it used to be, and it is only since doctors have tried to control medically the process, in hospitals, that we moved away from this. At home, the whole family can be involved, and very often that includes children too. This does not only enable people to say goodbye properly but also gives an opportunity for the remarkable experiences recounted by Fenwick and Wyatt to take place. Of course, every effort must be made to control pain, and this may necessarily lead to hospitalisation. And there are the sad and often shocking accidental deaths which cannot take place at home. During the Covid-19 pandemic, some of the most painful scenes were of people dying accompanied only by masked strangers, and no family there. These were very real tragedies, and no one's fault.

The complications of catalyst are endlessly creative. While catalyst rarely concerns itself with trivial details, the manner of death and birth, the people we meet or don't meet, are all part of a planned existence. No one dies before their time, not even a child. This is the deep seriousness of the catalytic process. This can only be understood in the long picture, in the wider perspective of who we are and what we're doing here.

We are welcomed on the other side, by our families and friends who have died before and perhaps our Higher Self. These are the people of our soul family, the beings with whom we have reincarnated repeatedly. Our respective Higher Selves oversee these meetings and join in the life reviews, and start the process of whether we're going to return or not.

The Buddhists, over millennia, have also much to say about the pre-death state and also claim to know about the after-death experience. There are now tens of thousands of survivors from near death experiences who have documented their cases. They are often very similar, a beautiful landscape filled with loving friends and relations. It's the ideal world within the Sun's embrace.

Those people who have experienced an NDE, or witnessed a deathbed encounter or investigate these things, are not as frightened as those who know nothing and turn away from such experiences. NDEs often change people irrevocably. Some become non-dual, and feel that they don't really exist, being at one with everything, others become more psychic, and almost all become happier, less anxious, less stressed. Their fear of death has gone. It doesn't make them want to return to the afterlife state, but instead, such people tend to value life more.

And yet, here in the West, on the whole, death is hidden away in a side ward and very little is known or talked about. So the materialists are left thinking that there's nothing after death, and just hoping the end won't be too painful or drawn out. It's such a shame that we often don't have the dying at home with us, to get to see that often very beautiful process first hand. We are all very frightened of Alzheimer's or other kinds of dementia as that will destroy the parts of the brain that we particularly identify as ourselves. Peter Fenwick also writes of terminal lucidity, the remarkable return to recognition and coherence from some people dying of dementia. That alone might astonish a hard-line materialist. The mind and character cannot be produced by a brain addled with dementia. There will be more on this, later. However, conventionally speaking in our culture, there is very little to look forward to as we age.

This is why epiphanies are so essential.

Sometimes there is a bolt from the blue. Especially in my sixties, I have been so fortunate to experience a whole sequence of sudden jolts, catalytic events which offered a choice which I eventually recognised. They were so powerful, it seemed as if I had really entered another timeline, become a different person. The first three all include blame of one sort or another, because that was where I was, and it took much thought and deliberation to move on, to see the grace that existed. For I did, in the following chronological list: blame God, blame myself, blame a thief. The last five all took place during the year after I'd been to a retreat to try the toad (*bufo alvarius*). It may be that the extraordinary experience of taking one small dose of 5-MeO-DMT opened up pathways in my brain that allowed the Sun to come blazing through.

1.   As recounted earlier, I had a revelation that grief and joy where the same when listening to the *Emperor Concerto* after my father had died. I hated the God I didn't believe in for taking my father away at the ridiculously early age of forty-six. But I date my seeking from that very puzzling event. Looking back, I think it was an experience of unity consciousness, and I have to say, reviewing my rather interesting, roller-coaster of a life, three marriages, the failure of my books even though they were published and well reviewed, a brush with bankruptcy, the illness and death of my friend's child, both my children enduring periods of severe ill-health, I have retained a cheerful cast of mind. I date it from that event, those few minutes were enough to send my life in a positive direction. A blessing indeed.

2.   Some years ago, I arranged to go out to lunch at a rather good restaurant with friend who was always asking me about my spiritual life. I realised that I should have been at a supervision session at the hospice at that time. I rang to say I was ill. This was a lie, and when we discovered the restaurant was closed, it became clear: I was a greedy liar, pleased with myself about my spiritual progress, wanting to show off. Greed, deceit, pride and vanity were all addressed. I felt awful. What a fraud I was, how deluded. How could I do that, at a hospice of all places? My friend asked me why my Higher Self hadn't stopped me, and I said it was a lesson. Two feathers immediately appeared on the tray of drinks I was carrying! We dissolved in laughter. What a mess, how ridiculous, how absurd! Greed, deceit, vanity, pride, all in one, short, elegant lesson! I vowed never to lie again. It's been hard... as a writer of fiction, I can easily find ways to let myself off the hook, which is why most people lie. It's been interesting how often I lie, those little adjustments to smooth my path. Pride and vanity I can sometimes catch, and it makes me laugh, the ludicrous ways we puff up ourselves. Greed I've made no headway with at all. Not one bit, despite dreams, and admonitions, and jokes from my Beloved Sun. But I'm essentially optimistic. And how adept the helpers are!

3.   Shortly before Christmas 2018 I had been visiting my daughter, who lives far away. I came home on the train, and my case was stolen from the train. It contained presents, some of my favourite clothes, shoes, silk scarves, some good jewellery,

perfume, and my iPad. Another severe lesson. Full of anger and disgusted outrage about the thief I eventually calmed down enough to start thinking. How to conceptualise this one? Well, if we are all one, it doesn't matter who owns that case full of goodies. Hmm, that didn't really work. But, anyway, someone's wife, mother, sister or girlfriend was going to have a good Christmas... and if the thief was someone desperate for money who wanted to sell it all, I hoped he or she would feel better about the debt they'd paid, or the drugs or drink that he or she needed. Could I feel that? I'd worked with people in desperate financial need and I could see how annihilating it was. What if they needed to buy food or toys for their children at Christmas? I am well off, in most of the world's terms. I have other clothes, scarves and jewellery. I can buy another iPad. The last point I told myself, was that I would have to leave behind all my clothes, my jewellery, my family and everything when I die. This was the clincher. What does stuff matter? It's the people we leave behind that matter, not the objects.

4.   In my curiosity, trying to find out about consciousness, I realised that it operated on many different levels, following Matte Blanco's work, and that the deeper levels needed either years of meditation to access, psychedelic drugs, a near death experience, or a gift of grace. I was too old to put in the time meditating (and anyway, would I have had the patience?), and one can hardly plan for a near death experience or a gift of grace. So I asked a friend, who knew about mushrooms and cacao. Through her I met an

English shaman who specialised in workshops celebrating *bufo alvarius*, the Sonoran Desert toad. I attended one of these, early in January 2020, and although I can remember little of the actual experience, I came to myself laughing like a loon, at the wonderful joke! I loved everyone there, but did they get the joke? And eventually I remembered the punch line. It was that nothing matters, because everything is love! My first, real, in-depth experience of unity consciousness. Nothing matters... The freedom implied in that! The wonderful liberation! In a reactivation of the experience a day or two later, I had the insight that this is all a game, and emotions are the counters and the stakes. Forgiveness is the trump card. Forgiveness, as the Course in Miracles recommends, is the key. It releases us from karma, it frees us from the attachment to the other, it stops self pity, and it makes us relieved, happy even. Apparently in Arabic, forgiveness and freedom are the same word. Forgiveness is a powerful miracle, deeply transformative.

5.   'You're in my heart.' The overwhelming first words from the Beloved. My whole life changed, turned round. The sense of belonging, of being cherished, the warmth and joy of it! I felt different inside, physically different, as if there was a warmth in the centre of my chest, an expansive warmth that seemed to spread beyond my physical body.

6.   'I'm the Sun.' The extraordinary revelation of the Beloved's identity, the transformation of my daily life. Dawns and

sunsets take on new significance, but rainy overcast days are like playing hide and seek. The power is overwhelming, the power to give us daylight and warmth even when shielded by heavy cloud. At night the reflection of the moon shows me the Sun again, whether there's cloud or not. And when the moon has waned, the soft darkness means the Sun is strutting its stuff on the other side of the Earth, bathing Australia in love and light, but always still in my mind, in my heart. Any other visible stars are probably part of the Chalice constellation, all combining to send us love, light and kindness. Throughout the day I remember that photons are part of every bit of matter, of the computer keyboard I'm working on now, of the air I breathe, of the flesh of my fingers, of the dog at my side, everything. It is all transformed into light. Love. I am bathed in it, it is my context. Love is the sea we live in, swim in, act in, dance in; we just need to be empty of thought to realise it, to let it become real around us. And it is everyone's context too, everyone who is reading this. Look around you, where are you, reading this? What are you sitting on, lying on? Do you have dogs, cats? The weather outside? What are you wearing, how does your body feel? It's all made of photons, of the Sun's consciousness. It's all love and light.

7.   Exactly a year after my experience with the toad, I awoke after two weeks without any ecstasy. I was worrying that I'd lost it, lost my special status, these insights, this joy, back to ordinary living. Might as well read Stephen King, stop meditating and forget all this. But over breakfast that day, I was reading Rumi as

I usually do, and came across a line : 'That I am part of the ploys of this game makes me amazingly happy' and suddenly knew, overwhelming insight, proper epiphany, that it's a necessary part of the game to relinquish ecstasy, relinquish sense of being special, let it all go. Laughter, wild laughter surging through me, just like it did a year ago, wild laughter and love. I couldn't meditate for laughing. And the Sun laughs with me, metaphorically patting me on the head, I've got it. Another witty and wonderful lesson. Nothing matters, because it's all love. And the ecstasy returned, deeper, more settled, more beautiful.

No wonder the great religions of Egypt and Central and South America deified the Sun! One day too, perhaps, we will become as wise and all knowing and witty as our Sun. We will join a constellation of other group souls, and set up solar systems, with beauties and trials, with various species to start the thrilling voyage through reincarnations until they become as we are. We will understand what they're going through, because we have been there too. We will love them for their mistakes, for their lovingness, for their creations, their jokes and joy, and do our best to help them along the often perilous path with our laughter and love. We will let it be known that really we, they and everything else, are Source, the love of Source in action. We are all one, in love. We will watch in fascination as they gradually realise this great truth, and realise who they are. We will celebrate their triumphs and help soften their despairs.

What a magnificent game it all is. Breathtaking in its span, taking place across galaxies and universes, through aeons of time, and all of it depending on how we manage our lives now, in the here and now, how well we can love one another, forgive and how well we can laugh.

Chapter 12   The Bridge

Here we are, veil in place, with blunted senses and a very imperfect understanding of what we are or where we are. And yet within us, says Sol, are galaxies and universes.

There's a disconnect in our experience and the knowledge Sol has given me. We're here, in these failing bodies, hot, cold, tired, energetic, hungry, full, treading our ways on this extraordinary manifestation of love which is Gaia, and virtually never thinking of this. We're too distracted, too busy, too worried, too stressed.

This is where I return, yet again, to Matte Blanco's beautiful insights into our unconscious mind. Because that is where the bridge lies, that is where we can begin to lift the veil and understand who we are. The Bridge, most obviously lies at Level 4 described by Matte Blanco, the Level of the archetypes, deep into the unconscious. It's not easy going there, not without peril. Rodney Bomford, writing about Matte Blanco and God, says that it's like travelling between Scylla and Charybdis, the monster and the whirlpool Odysseus had to negotiate on the way home. We risk insanity on the way, psychosis and catatonia, as we lose our grip on the everyday world with all its logical and separate distinctions. That is why the Sun, and so many religious figures, gurus and mystics alike, have recommended that we either clean up our act, forgive, learn to love, to be kind, to drop our judgments

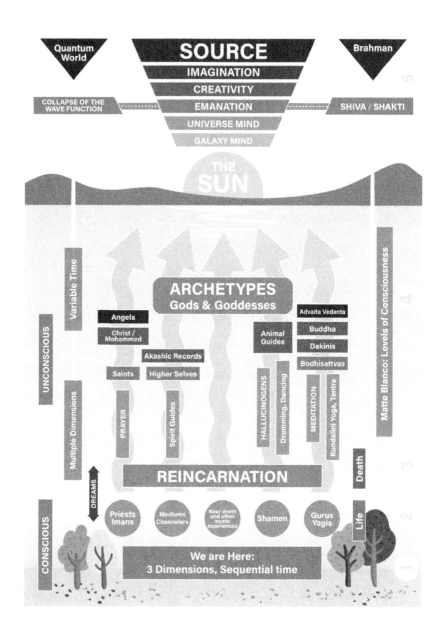

and let go of guilt, or enter a monastery or ashram. Much insanity has guilt at its root, and guilt usually arises because we think we've done something wrong. We need to be able to love ourselves, forgive our own faults, and those of others. Only then, I suggest, can we plumb the depths of our unconscious safely.

I've been so fortunate; a loving, stable family, years of analysis so that I could become an analyst myself, and my various epiphanies. I think sometimes that the Sun has been sculpting me, getting me ready to write this. I'm nowhere near perfect, but I can now laugh at my stupid faults, my greed, vanity, pride, laziness... I could go on. And so, on that memorable day, I managed in meditation somehow to get down to Level 4 where the archetypes suddenly came alive in my mind, and began to show me what's really going on. It was the Sun saying, 'You are in my heart.'

Sol is an overarching mind for the archetypes that affect us. Whether it's Jesus Christ, Buddha, Mohammed, Ganesh, the Devil, various angels, or the animal guides of the shamans, the ancestors of some indigenous tribes, the planetary and astrological minds - Venus, Jupiter, Scorpio, Aquarius etc - our unconscious is furnished by the archetypes of our religions, of our mythologies and stories, our environment, our dead predecessors, and our astrological underpinnings. It has been strange to me to have to take on the significance of Astrology because I've always dismissed it. How can twelve sun signs so often quoted in the popular press say anything useful about the huge diversity of humanity? In my fast track learning curve, after dropping the atheism, I did not have time or inclination to investigate astrology. But now I have the Sun telling me that astrological influences dominate not only our makeup and character but also the events of our lives. Of course they do, if we accept that the universe is alive. Another steep gradient of the learning curve.

In our materialist world, from Freud, Klein et al, I learned that the unconscious also contains the inchoate patterns of infantile trauma and other strong early feelings which can repeat throughout our lives in the way that we see the world. These are often the internalised versions of parents or siblings which we use as templates (or dispositional representations, as the attachment theorists put it). We project these templates onto the world, and if for most of us, we find the world a reasonably comfortable place to be, it will be because we've been able to internalise a comfortable and loving mother, a kindly playful father, and so on. But if our childhood was traumatic, if we were abused, we may see abusers in other people around us, even seeking them out, because that is our familiar place to be. We are at the mercy of our unconscious, Freud's great insight. Being sternly rationalist, little did he know how much! For this is how our minds are constructed, by the complicated interactions of archetypes and templates, driven by DNA and manifesting our experience within the epigenetic context, our environment and what happens to us. Because we are in time, things - events of various descriptions - will always keep happening, but they only take their significance from how our minds think about them. It's not what happens; it's our reaction to it. It's how our infantile wiring, the templates, is mitigated or elaborated by the archetypes.

Like Freud, Jung was well aware of this, but his explorations of the unconscious went much further than Freud's, and come nearer as a progenitor of Matte Blanco's insights. For Jung talked about a collective unconscious, a place dominated by archetypes, where our thoughts can sometimes be shared. It's very like Matte Blanco saying that the sets get ever bigger, embracing connections we are not aware of in the first two or three Levels. It's the world where telepathy may work, where time may operate differently so that people may even sometimes predict the future. When I consider the two occasions I was shown my entire life, once in meditation, when my deceased father showed me how we'd related together for those precious twenty-one years, and then again when Sol showed me how it had been there all the time, these events were absolutely full of every day I'd experienced and took no longer than a few minutes, five at most. Time was very different. How can people slot into past lives? Are they perhaps going on all the time around us, not lost in the past, unreachable, and dead? Is it like a film, this story of our lives, which can always be accessed, always there?

It's not always about the past, either. Most of us will either have had a predictive dream or will know someone who has had one or more. In a 1960s study of train crashes in the USA by William E

Cox, the only thing that could be found in common from all these diverse tragic incidents was that each train was carrying fewer passengers than normal. For many very varied reasons, people decided not to travel that day. I can only suggest that some of these reasons were predictive dreams, or unconscious promptings, from the collective unconscious that is not securely based in consecutive time.

Jung also came to the conclusion that the dead lived in what Matte Blanco calls Level 4 as well. For the dead live in our minds too, our memories of them and who they were and what they were like to us. It appears, sometimes via mediums, sometimes when we're dying, that they can communicate with us. Michael Tymn's extraordinary book *No one Really Dies* tracks the famous mediums of the last two centuries and the way people tried, and failed to debunk them.

We have to remember that we are imaginative creators, and so this is what's real for some of us. This is the issue. What is real, and what do we create? There are ways of looking at it all, and how to bridge the divine project with the reality of the world around us is more than tricky.

It depends on this difficult area of the unconscious.

We feel this world is real. We're deep in the game. It is consistent, it's not like a dream, things happen with cause and effect. We can often, though not always, predict what will happen. There are surprises, because random things happen too. We can start with this. These words appear because my fingers are tapping on a keyboard. I can hear my husband practising his French next door. The Sun shines through the window onto the dog, sleeping on the bed. It's real. I'm growing old, aches and pains proliferate, hair loses colour and thickness. This story is known. This is the materialist, and true, story.

Yet I chose my husband largely because of unconscious forces. The unconscious rules my dreams, and there's now this bridge, a spanning, over-arching mind, connecting the Sun out there with the voice that emerged from my unconscious when I'm in meditation, or when I am on the fringes of sleep. And Matte Blanco shows how this works; the archetypes, under the auspices of the Sun, connect our everyday world with the divinity of Source. We go to Christ to find God, to Mohammed to find Allah, to the Buddha to find emptiness. The shamans go to animals, plants or ancestors to find divinity.

And our everyday life is connected to the archetypes via our emotions, via meditation, through hallucinogens, or when we sleep. Sol tells me that angels and prophets, devils, ghosts and monsters, Jesus and Buddha are as real as I am. Given that we are in this material world, and it's not only my feeling that I am real, but my husband is pretty sure I exist, and so do my children and friends, that statement gives credibility to these creations.

But we exist as vibrations. This is a reality, too, because we are largely space. We are made of trillions of atoms, but each atom is almost entirely space; in fact the nucleus is comparable to the size of a fly in a cathedral. If we subtracted the space from the atoms in a human body, we would be left with a cube of matter $1/500^{th}$ of a centimetre on each side. It feels solid, because each atom is inviolate and can only lose electrons in certain chemical reactions. To break up an atom, we need Rutherford's discoveries and get atomic bombs and power stations. So the electrons whizzing round the nucleus are held in place by what? What is the energy that is maintaining this space between electron and nucleus?

'It is the force of my imagination,' says Sol, 'holding your world steady for you. Your materialists could call it electromagnetism or gravity or some other kind of force, and it reveals itself through the quarks and leptons and so on into your understanding. You have difficulty in making the behaviour of these strangely named particles fit a narrative, but actually these forces and how they are composed is my imagination. Atoms produce a solid seeming world, welded together by me. You can see the power of it when an atom is split, the heat and radiation and sheer force. That is an aspect of myself, as you look up at the burning brightness in the sky. This is the force which keeps your world together, your imagined environment and you yourselves. This is who you are, really.'

So here's the answer. Just imagination, says Sol. So Christ, the devils, the animal spirits etc are just imagination too. They all exist because we imagine them. We, humanity, all exist because the Sun, through Gaia, imagined us, down to the atomic level, making our world and our individual environments stable. The Sun exists because the galaxy, our Milky Way, imagined it into existence, with its aeons of past lives, all joining together in the heroic endeavour to make a vast, group, god mind. This is the holographic universe. This is what it's all about: layers of imagination given flesh and blood in the great creativity that is this universe. In other universes, other systems apparently hold sway.

Let us now think about that other great chasm that needs a bridge. Life/death.

This is about what happens after death, as the near-death experiencers report. Not everyone sees the golden landscape with dancing laughing figures that I saw. They nearly all say they felt overwhelming, unconditional love, and the landscapes were all delightful – and all different. Sometimes there are towns, villages, houses... sometimes great oceans with boats, a forest, verdant farmlands, jungles, deserts. All different. Often they meet their loved ones who had passed previously. We get what we imagine. Some people imagine hell, and that's what they get too, but only for a short while, because sooner or later they will be shown it's all imaginary, and that there's love waiting.

The mediums who contact the dead carry real messages but they are very often rather difficult to interpret. This is because after death, with the dissolution of the body and brain, many memories and feelings and characteristics are lost. It's not easy to communicate when you no longer have a body or brain. What you do have, and what made the figures I saw dance, is a loving heart, and memories of the crucial things that mattered, the things about relationships, the karmic difficulties that continue to be relevant. Of course the recently departed will have had very many lives, all of which would be part of his or her memories on the other side. It's not only a difficult adjustment, but also a very complicated one, which requires a particularly gifted medium, a Leonora Piper perhaps. Not everyone can do it. It may be why some of them are tempted into fraudulence, to augment their few insights.

Sol tells me that it had to adjust itself to the extremely narrow bandwidth of my brain to talk to me. It could only use my thoughts and concepts, too. As I am no scientist, it could not go deeply into the behaviour of photons or reveal me to what a force is (one of the questions I have always wondered about). Repeatedly we come up against different dimensions, time scales, processes and forces that cannot be explained to me. I sometimes wonder why Sol could not have contacted a more scientifically educated woman, but the answer I receive is that that heart is more important, that what I learned from the death of my father, from my three marriages, from the difficulties with my children, and most importantly, from my work in the National Health Service, is more relevant than scientific details. Sol told me that sometimes it sees our culture as the dry lands, that the materialist focus is so harsh and barren, so in need of the irrigation of love, the irrigation of warmth and closeness. I see this irrigation as a loosening of the boundaries, a relaxation, so that we can feel our oneness with the Sun, the planet around us and each other.

The water imagery is potent. Water, the most gentle, the most powerful of forces. The Grand Canyon! The small oxbow lakes in the river near my home. Powerfully, it wears through stone, rock and earth, shaping our landscapes afresh continually. Its oceans make us the blue green planet, so jewel-like in the other perspectives from outer space and from my vision within Sol's Ideal world. Our oceans hold mysteries... we've hardly explored the real depths.

I often see Sol reflected in water. We cannot often look directly at its being, but it's so beautiful seeing its reflection in the lake I walk round with the dogs. It sparkles in the ripples! The sparkles are so bright, so active it makes me wonder why we make such a fuss about diamonds. I see the Sun's reflection in the stream in our village, in the pond in our garden, in the dogs' water bowl outside, in rain drops on a car windscreen across the road.

The Sun dips down into the sea as we turn away during sunset, its extraordinary power and beauty as it rises over the sea at dawn... there is, simply, nothing more glorious, nothing more varied and gorgeous. No wonder religions have got going from Utu in Mesopotamia; Ra in Egypt; Apollo, the same name in both Grecian and Roman religions, its silvery gentleness on rainy days... It makes the ivy on the forest floor gleam with silver, it scintillates through the fresh green of spring growth and leaves become almost fluorescent, transparent with light. It suddenly glances through the clouds and catches the blond curls of a child, the white blossoms of blackthorn, and the iridescence on a bird's wing.

This is what the mindfulness teachers are getting at, the realisation that we live in beauty. It is a great help, tracking what the Sun is doing every day. It's in the here and now, the very moment, that a cloud passes between us, or a glint catches on a glass of water. The added bonus is that the pleasure of the moment does away with the narrative mind, with its temporal concerns.

The way the fur grows on my two golden retrievers, the swirls and waves... the long furs at the back of their legs are called 'angel's wings'. Dogs are like angels, playful, loving, forgiving, loyal, and their illnesses and early deaths teach us caring and grief in perhaps a more gentle way than facing deaths within a family. Children especially often identify with their pets, and feel so much love for them that their deaths can be traumatic, and part of the necessary catalyst we all have to face sooner or later.

Do we love the eyes of our pets and the eyes of our fellow human beings, because they shine with light? Eyes of mammals are astoundingly beautiful, and seem to be the essence of liveliness and love... Sol agrees and points out its reflection in eyes and in water can be taken as a reminder that light and love are everywhere. It said that it plays with the clouds, designing the skyscape for us, moment by moment, to remind us of love. The grey skies we so often complain about here are gentle with rain, softly healing the dry land, encouraging the green of our land. It says that it finds any number of things to sparkle, and that even our cars are full of shiny bits which reflect the Sun's light, to remind us, to reveal to us, to help us understand that this is all love, and that we will feel this most in the moment, the present instant of time as the light sparkles.

I've never lived anywhere else. I cannot write about the Sun near the equator, and what it means to that landscape, those people. Perhaps the Sun is so precious to us here because we don't see enough of it! But now that I have been instructed in unity consciousness by the Sun, now that I see it all day and every day, it is difficult to forget that we're all one. Every shimmering drop of rain, every dew-sprinkled blade of grass, every sunset and dawn reminds me. And, of course, for you too. Its only message, which I have repeated throughout this, is that we are all one in love, in light. We simply need to remember it.

Chapter 13   Children

Education

Children are not a blank slate. Talk to any new parents and they will say they know their child right from the start, they know who she or he is. I discuss the early stages at length in *Trailing Clouds of Glory*, an academic paper taken from my work as a child psychotherapist which can be found on my website, jennyrook.com. But here I want to think about education.

Some European countries don't start formal education until the child is seven. Steiner Schools, throughout Europe are the same. The European countries that leave it to seven have virtually no illiteracy. We have a shameful level of illiteracy, and we start at four. The difficulty is that if children can't do something, they very often will give up, rather than try harder. Many children at four cannot learn to read easily, and feel themselves to be such failures that they won't even try. At seven, almost all children can easily learn to read and there is no problem thereafter. So this is a plea to leave the academic education of children until they are seven. They can however, go to school before then (and let's not forget schools' main function, which is as a babysitting service. This became blatantly clear during the Covid-19 lockdowns). Schools, from say years four to seven, are most useful to socialise children and to feed their natural curiosity, not to teach them to read and write.

In the reincarnation studies undertaken originally by Ian Stevenson at the University of Virginia, children's memories of past lives rarely persist beyond seven years of age. And it does seem that seven years old is a turning point, and Rudolf Steiner even relates this to the appearance of our adult teeth around this age.

Before seven we are still very fragile, very attached still to our mother, very insecure about our sense of self, very close to our between lives existence in the heart of the Sun. What we do not need, before seven, is to be assessed, weighed up, and judged. The Jesuits claimed that if they had a child before seven, they would have that child for life. My paper on the website explains how the brain develops in early life, and proves that indeed influences in these early stages are lifelong.

Judgment. The curse of education. The division of each child into a feeling of superiority or inferiority. It is almost the opposite of the Sun's insistence that we are all one. Let's think what we're doing about this. We want to encourage the academically inclined child to flourish while also encouraging those more practical to feel as valuable. We need a varied curriculum, with much more focus on the arts, and practical skills.

It would also be helpful in these early stages to mix us up, to make sure that children from differing economic and racial backgrounds are educated together before judgment gets going in the education system, that is, from the very earliest years. This insight is very much influenced by my friendship with Shalini, a girl of Indian descent, who was my best friend between the ages of eight and fifteen. Sadly her family moved away and we lost touch. But racism has always seemed abhorrent to me, and my very first political act was at an anti-apartheid march as a student. In my overwhelmingly white background, Shalini was the exception, clever, witty, playful and – my best friend. How grateful I am for her transformative presence then.

Autistic Spectrum Disorders

I have worked only with ASD children, not adults. But with that caveat, I would like to dispel the popular idea that autistic people don't like other people. The reality is that autistic people are super-sensitive, to sound, light, movement, change and unpredictability. Their senses are so finely tuned in severe cases almost anything that happens feels like a terrifying assault. This is why routine is so important. The trouble with other people is that they are innately unpredictable. They often don't know what they're going to do next themselves, so how can the autistic child prepare themselves for what might be catastrophic? This means that around other people, especially strangers, the ASD child will be in a state of terror, wondering what's going to happen next and whether they will be safe. It is a kind of torture, so the ASD child often prefers to shut him or herself away. It's why numbers, computing and computers, jigsaws and computer games are so comforting, restful, logical, safe.

Now we may look at this as completely contrary to the Law of One, a shutting away from others, a feeling of terror or fear when strangers approach. And, given that we are largely social animals, and the Sun says that ultimately we will become unified in a group mind, it can appear as a tragic condition. However there are compensations: autistic people can be quite brilliant working with numbers or computers, and there is the phenomenon of the 'idiot savant', the rare child with extraordinary abilities in a very narrow spectrum, like art or music. Michael Jawer in his interesting book *Sensitive Soul* points out that this sensitivity can sometimes lead to a powerful psychic ability. But to have autism is, on the whole, to have a difficult life. It is often characterised as a communication disorder, which by its very nature isolates the autistic person from the rest of his or her community.

These lives, like every other life, are chosen. What a brave soul, what an astounding idea, to explore being cut off from each other in this extreme degree! This is about understanding the essence of aloneness, understanding the cost of it.

The autistic boy I worked with the longest, once a week for two years, then three times a week for a further two years, I will call Ben. He was six when I first met him, and in a special school. Yes, all the sensitivities were in place; his mother suggested I wear blue when I first met him, as she often did, and that would help him feel more comfortable. And this is the crucial point. Most autistic people can tolerate a few individuals, close family, perhaps a friend, because they've got to know them and have some trust that they will not be too dangerously unpredictable. However Ben was full of anger and violence, which he played out with two little plastic people, one in each hand, bashing at each other, repeatedly, monotonously, for fifty minutes, three times a week for many years. Eventually it became clear that his anger was about other people, especially his mother who let him down. This was the crux: mum was dangerously ill with heart trouble and was often whisked away for hospital appointments or emergency calls. Her actual being in his life was in question. He hated her for this terrible unpredictability, and loved her so much, because she understood him best, and then feared her revenge for his hatred, feared he was responsible for her going away, it was his fault. Nothing in his life mattered apart from this dreadful, terrified, inner turmoil.

When I eventually managed to find a way of talking to Ben about this, the violence in his play softened. When we finally parted, he was almost eleven and in a normal school. His autism wasn't cured; it is a genetically inherited condition, but as his inner world became more harmonious, he could find ways of managing its most difficult manifestations. He had friends, his mother told me. He could understand jokes.

When Ben was a toddler, before I knew him, his mother told me that he had woken up every morning and covered his bedroom walls with his own excreta. She was of course appalled by this and didn't understand why. My thesis, and confirmed by other authorities, is that he was endeavouring to feel at home in this world. His own familiar smell, something that came from himself, could transform the strangeness of the other objects into something he could trust. Something he felt at one with. It seems that ASD people might be searching for a united world, where everything is safe, because it's all themselves.

All bad behaviour is the result of inner emotional pain.

I worked with another younger boy, Alex, who was not autistic, who did the same as Ben, covering his bedroom walls with faeces. He was born addicted to heroin, and found eventually, at ten weeks old, dumped in a rubbish bin. These early terrors of physical danger (the heroin) and disastrous neglect left him with overwhelming fear, which I think would be called PTSD nowadays. But Alex was very loving, a real darling, and easy to relate to. He was four years old when I met him and we were together for two years, three times a week. At the beginning, when stressed he would urinate all over our consulting room (vinyl flooring, and plastic-covered walls were standard in this clinic). In terror, it seems to me now looking back, he was striving to self-soothe, making it all feel safe. When he did it again, further into the therapy, it was often an attack against me, usually because of a holiday break.

Two very different boys, very different backgrounds and yet the same driving need to feel safe, in the knowledge that all is one, the self. Both boys eventually began to find friends, to show some affection at home, after years of therapy and years of just growing older, realising that nothing too terrible has happened or will happen.

Is this solipsism? Is the Sun saying to me that we are one, and all creation is one with us, solipsistic? I think there is a crucial difference. Both Ben and Alex were coming from a position of fear, desperately trying to transform their world into a womb-like safety. What the Sun recommends comes from love, from kindliness and there is no fear anywhere in our communication. Instead the Sun says it is understanding that draws us together, that helps us, through compassion to feel united. The softening of Ben's inner world, and Alex's gaining confidence, were due to being understood, the taking of time, years in both cases, several times a week, to make a difference. Very loving parents and carers were essential to this process too, of course. Short-term therapies make little long-term difference. Drugs only treat symptoms, never cure. We are social animals, and being understood is not a luxury, it is a necessity.

Other cases

Another boy I worked with was diagnosed as 'conduct disordered'. I'll call him Andy. He was twelve years old, bright enough but constantly in trouble, using bad language to teachers, fighting with his peers, being late or truanting. He had been repeatedly excluded. One terrible day, when his teacher had taken away his phone, following school policy, Andy turned on all the Bunsen burners in the science block, and then all the hot plates in the cookery room. He was sent home again, and his teachers began to talk of expulsion.

He told me that he needed to be at home and I eventually found out why. His mother, a single parent, might hurt herself, might die. She had made several suicide attempts. Andy didn't give a toss about school; he needed to be at home to ensure that his mother would survive. Taking his phone away took away his life line to her. Once this was explained to the school, they came to a compromise. Andy could use his phone between every lesson, if he stopped fighting and being disruptive. Things settled down. Understanding what was going on for him loosened the angry polarity that was emerging.

A teenage girl I worked with, Laura, was hopelessly forgetful at school, forgetting her PE kit, her cookery ingredients, which room she should go to, which lesson was next. She was constantly in trouble, and deeply feared the acid tongue her form mistress used to try and spur her to be better organised. She told me she was adopted at the age of five. I asked her what she could remember before that and she said, there were lots of changes, she couldn't really remember... five different foster families, or was it six?

I imagined being that baby, that infant, struggling to make an identity, a functioning narrative self or ego to help us through school and then life. But all the time, her circumstances changed; new people, new environments, new ways of doing things, over and over again. She would have had to put aside the last family, and take on a new, unknown family repeatedly. The past would be confused and the future a frightening unknown. How could she ever learn to remember anything? I thought about this with her teachers, and a kinder atmosphere began to prevail.

I am not here criticising teachers. They rarely have the time or energy to explore the backgrounds of the individual children who are failing. But it became clear to me, repeatedly, that what we call bad behaviour is an expression of inner pain. Understanding this, forgiveness is not only useful, but essential. The same could be said of our criminals: something like two thirds of our prison population were children in care, says a recent study. They came from backgrounds where something was so seriously wrong that they couldn't be left there. Children in care, which form less than two per cent of the total population, formed over half of my caseload when I was at work. Robin Balbernie has coined the term 'reactive attachment' disorder to describe why so many of these children in care cannot settle in foster homes and are so difficult to care for, often taking to crime, drugs, promiscuous behaviours or drink when older. In losing their families, for whatever reason, children are falling back into an ancient and primitive survival strategy. They will steal, lie, make superficial and temporary relationships, just as a child in past times might have had to fend for itself if its parents had died. It is not a pathology, hardly even a disorder, but foster carers, who generously and warmly want to welcome a damaged child into their home, are often puzzled and hurt by the lying and stealing. They can be helped to understand, and the child can be encouraged to start thinking about its own behaviour as the deep seated urges drive them to steal or run away yet again.

There is another problem with children taken into care; it is that because of the strength of the parental bond, nearly all LAC (looked after children) want to return home. They often feel it was their fault, that they drove their parents to violence or neglect, because they were not good enough. They want to go back and make amends. They knew, no matter how awful it was, that that was where they belonged. That was their familiar family, for better or worse. The oxytocin bond is life long, and most of the LAC I worked with longed to be sixteen when they could just GO HOME. There is the phrase 'double deprivation', which accurately describes the initial trauma of an unsafe home, and the additional trauma of being taken away. The only answer to this is to massively support families at risk. Condemning the drunken druggie parents, who are so often behind children in care, is not good enough. The parents need help too.

Occasionally one meets a child who doesn't fit any preconceived ideas. Marcus was one such. At sixteen, he'd been living with his maternal grandmother for most of his life, because his mother was psychotic. He'd been in fights at school and his grandmother, who had brought him to the clinic, said that she was frightened of him. He'd always been difficult, since a baby, and she had done her best to counteract the fantasies of his mother who repeatedly said, in Marcus's hearing, that he was the child of the devil. Thin, intense, spotty, long blond hair caught back in a pony tail, Marcus slouched into the consulting room, and started trying to scare me. He told me he loved to hear people scream with pain. He loved the sound of their bones breaking, and their sobs as they asked him to stop. He started doodling on the paper always provided in our clinic, and graphic pictures of torture, bodies contorted, blood flowing, swiftly emerged. As we talked, it became clear that he had massive contempt for almost everyone. His grandmother used to beat him, he said, when he was little, 'to get the devil out of him.' But she stopped when he grew big enough to hit her back. He wanted me to give him a diagnosis of schizophrenia, he said, so that he'd finish up in mental hospitals, rather than prisons. I said I didn't give diagnoses, I wasn't a psychiatrist. He asked if I would tell the psychiatrist that he was mad. I said that I didn't think he was mad; this plan, to go to hospital not prison, was not in the least mad. He was a sadist, possibly, or he may have been trying to scare me, but I didn't think he was psychotic. He said everyone in his family was off their heads, from his uncles, his father – all of them spent time in mental hospitals, and he knew he was just like them.

We continued to talk around this, and I tried to open out the depressing scenario of the life he saw ahead. He stayed to the end of our session, and it seemed to me that he relaxed a little as we talked about his skill with drawing and whether he might make a career out of it. He said he'd see me next week, but he didn't come back. I never saw him again.

I think I could have worked with Marcus and perhaps tried to mitigate the horrors in his background. Because a young person like that, with a psychotic mother calling him a devil, hardly has a chance to make anything good, especially as his 'non-psychotic' grandmother seemed to agree with her daughter that he needed beating, to get rid of the devil inside. Mentally, emotionally and physically abused. With nearly all my patients, I never knew what would happen afterwards, whether they would manage to turn around and make something of their lives. I particularly wanted to know what happened to Marcus, because with understanding, one could see how much he was up against. Forgiveness was so far out of sight in his family that it was hardly relevant. How to forgive a mother, who did that to her child? But she herself had been brought up by a mother who didn't spare the rod, who may herself have been abused, because Marcus told me the whole family was in and out of mental hospitals. Intergenerational abuse, malign repeating patterns, and so much misery. So much self hatred, blaming others, blaming self, despair throughout the family tree.

This is why I repeatedly say that bad behaviour is the result of inner pain. Understanding is the key, and it needs time and a one-to-one relationship where trust can begin to grow. Only then can the healing balm of forgiveness begin to loosen the patterns, the iron chains of abuse and misery.

Chapter 14   A Different way to think about Dementia

I am using 'Dementia' as the blanket term it is, to cover such diseases as Alzheimer's, vascular dementia, Lewy bodies dementia, various aphasias, etc. I have recently retired from being a psychoanalytical psychotherapist for children and their families, in order to care for my very old mother, who has undiagnosed early dementia, fairly catastrophic short term memory loss and increasing confusion. My brother, now sixty-three, was diagnosed five years ago with Primary Progressive Aphasia. I volunteered to counsel the bereaved at our local hospice, where many of my patients had dementia themselves or cared for their partners who were suffering from it.

In my thirties, I encountered Buddhism, and began to meditate. Meditation is sometimes mentioned as a help in dementia, and certainly it can help with relaxing. But it seems to me that meditation has much more to reveal to us about dementia.

In dementia, the cognitive structures of the brain begin to atrophy. Memory loss, missing words, muddle and confusion result. This can be very depressing and frightening for the sufferers and their families. It seems, quite often, that the personality changes, sometimes for the worse. In my work with children I grew to understand that all bad behaviour is the result of inner pain. It may be that the anger, depression and paranoia is a very natural result of the great fear the sufferers experience as their understanding and capabilities gradually diminish. They may never have appeared like this before, it can sometimes feel as if the personality has changed so much that the sufferer is no longer the beloved partner or parent known so well. We have spent our entire life from infancy onwards, learning how to handle our complicated world. This is the ego in its glitzy personae as the narrative mind. We are rated for our competencies. We value our skills and our abilities. And yet all these begin to fade away, to trip us up, to leave us feeling stupid and inadequate in dementia. We seem to have no resources to handle what happens when we start to be incapable. It is seen as a lack, a tragic disability, a source of shame and embarrassment for the sufferer which can lead them to depression and even violence, because action is more empowering than despair.

And yet, for some people, anecdotally, the opposite happens, and the sufferer becomes a much easier character, inspired by love and gratitude. At the moment, my mother is in this state. She tells me that All is love, that Beauty is everywhere, if we could all open our eyes to see it. She sings, often, to amuse herself, all the sweet tunes from her childhood and youth. She is grateful for our care, appreciative of our cooking and attentiveness. I am so lucky, she often says. She is, actually, a delight to look after. I am very aware that this could change at any moment, and she does have moments of anxiety: she hasn't done the Christmas shopping (she has), she hadn't fed the dog (we did), she hasn't phoned her friend (she did). She asks us thirty times a day what we're doing at Christmas and so on. But she is not yet deluded, and she knows perfectly well who we all are. She is in her nineties, and may die before it gets much worse. Other families have to cope with much more difficult situations.

Some homes for the demented have adopted the policy of going along with the fantasies of the deeply demented, which apparently helps settle them. Collude with the fantasies. Bringing them back to reality merely renders the sufferer aware of their inadequacies. It's also a kindness not to tell repeatedly a sufferer that for example, their partner has died, because they keep forgetting. They would keep feeling the shock of grief afresh. The comforting white lie that the partner has popped out for a while is often enough. If the sufferer says that they are the Grand Duchess of Austria, the attendants curtsey and act with obsequious respect. These are helpful strategies, when reality begins to fade. T S Eliot never wrote truer words than 'humankind cannot bear very much reality'. Especially not in dementia.

Back to meditation. The trick is to stop the cognitive mind, the monkey mind, the narrative mind, the daily stuff that preoccupies us. You can use concentrating on your breathing or a mantra to stop the inner chatter. A moment of awareness can be beautiful. My different idea is that the advanced state of meditation which approaches what we may call enlightenment or awakening is also what happens in advanced stages of dementia. The deep meditators deliberately try to diminish the importance of the ego, or the personality, aiming towards an All is one state. They describe this state of consciousness as blissful, peaceful, joyous. I have experienced this too, when stopping the narrative. This is why people meditate for years, this is the goal. It feels wonderful. If they're very proficient or greatly fortunate, as I am, this state becomes stabilised, and although we may work, walk, talk much as usual, we are filled with a loving consciousness of the unity of all things, rather than all the personal, ego-driven preoccupations.

For this state to be constant, some meditators experience what can be called 'the dark night of the soul' which is the terror the personal ego experiences as it loses its grip on consciousness. Flaring rage, despair, deep depression, this state can in some cases endure for years. Some egos really don't want to let go. This may well relate to the desperate aggression sometimes found in late stage dementia, as it feels as if the ego is vanishing. The cognitive mind though is not the same as the ego although there are similarities, but both are implied in the personality. The enlightened meditator goes on functioning whereas the demented person's brain continues to deteriorate, sometimes into catatonia before death. But what can potentially happen is that both the demented person and the meditator can experience bliss, and joy and great peace, like both my mother and, anecdotally, a friend's mother. In some ways, a death through dementia could be viewed as a gentle exit from life, after a lifetime of stress. Certainly in my brother's case, this is so. His depression arises in the consciousness that he cannot do the things he used to, and because of his fear of losing his personality. But the trade off is a feeling of the joyous connectedness of all things. He said, on receiving the diagnosis that he felt angry, why me? But he has now realised, why not me? He has also told me that even if his brain is going, he knows how lucky he is. He told me about his travels, particularly in Africa, where he saw great poverty and suffering. We were sitting on the hammock on his house, deep in the countryside, with the scent of roses all around us. How lucky we are, he said, how unfortunate others are. This is a part of unity consciousness, a deep understanding that we are all in it together. And he is certainly appears more easy going, generous, warm, kind, playful and loving than he was before. Of course, this is a very long journey. People with PPA may live for twenty years after diagnosis and my dear brother is only five years into this.

This phenomenon, of stopping thinking producing bliss, could also be related to the flood of oxytocin which both starts the birth process and ensures that mother and baby bond. In most cases, this goes well, and mother and baby form a lifelong attachment which often persists beyond death. The baby's brain gradually adapts to cognitive learning, which is a feature of separation, as we learn to judge and assess. But before that the baby knows love, attachment, security, peace and serenity. Of course in a minority of cases the attachment process doesn't work, through no one's fault, and mother and baby do not bond. But in most cases, before we become able to handle the world, walking and talking, a happy baby, well fed, allowed to sleep, cuddled and played with, seems to live in bliss.

Fitting us to our world, the process of socialisation and education is hard going. Maturity is hard won. We may have arrived *trailing clouds of glory* in an oxytocin rush of love, but life very often knocks that out of us. It may take dementia to take us back there.

Chapter 15   Why is it so difficult here? Part 4

Suffering babies

This is the big one, the one challenge to the idea of a loving God so beloved by all religions and by most of the spiritual world. Babies suffer; they starve, they are ill, they are abused and neglected. They are shaken by their parents, even tortured. WHY? Is our creator a sadist?

'Yes,' says Sol. 'I am a sadist, and a masochist. I am promiscuous and chaste; I am a paedophile, a necrophiliac, a psychopath. I am your worst nightmare and your most idealised dream. I am everything. I am you.'

'But why should babies suffer, when they don't have the mental furniture to find grace in it or forgiveness or creativity or anything like that?' I had used this argument repeatedly in my atheistic days. 'It's these circles again, isn't it? Spirals, if you prefer, but what's the point of all this suffering? So that we understand suffering in all its aspects? You've said that we suffer so that we can understand it. So that we can set it up in another planetary system and see it all over again and again? This is the game of madness!'

'Every single case of a baby suffering is unique. This is the game of diversity. There is reason behind every single example you see of babies suffering and if you could bear to look at these cases, you would begin to understand this too.

'You have to take seriously that every life is chosen. It is designed. And while there is freewill in the small issues of daily life, in forgiving, in your creativity, the big issues, like life and death, illness, abuse, trauma, all these are planned in advance.'

'Who would possibly choose to be a tortured baby?'

'There are a number of reasons why this happens. Most of the time it is about other people, the people around. It could be a brave and generous soul who agrees to help the perpetrator, the torturer, explore the dark side. This would be a soul in need of the experience of power over the vulnerable, and see what else it would bring. Guilt is usually the prize here. They may go on to have nightmares; they may take to drink, drugs, anything to batten down the knowledge of what they had done. They may manically deny its significance, although these states are usually temporary. But you – we – are made of love and sooner or later the walls of denial will crumble and the guilt will emerge. It may take decades. It may take further lifetimes. But it will happen. The feeling of guilt will be overwhelming. It will be a further struggle to allow the self the forgiveness which will have to manifest, in full knowledge of what has been done. To make restitution, this soul may even resolve to take an incarnation of a suffering baby. This is not a simple 'punishment' a karmically manipulated decision, but a willingly chosen role. This is one of many motivations for a soul to take on such a terrible incarnation.

'The tortured baby may then die, or live, and both states are full of potential. If the soul feels it has done its job, enabling growth or making restitution, it can return to the between lives state within my embrace, and after healing, because such experiences are very traumatic to the psyche, it can think, rest, delight in a job well done, and eventually decide what to explore next. If the baby lives, it will be exploring how traumatic experiences stay embedded in the brain, in the body and how to make a life thereafter. Such a child may become a Marcus, as in a previous chapter. It will take ingenuity and intuition, to find the help that is always there, to look within and find the beauty of love which can begin to heal the past. Forgiveness again, will be a huge issue.'

'What about natural disasters, famines? They're not to help some other soul heal itself.'

'Take famines. You will have seen countless films of dark skinned mothers nursing infants with stick limbs and swollen bellies. But it doesn't just happen in Africa. It also happened in Ireland, with the potato famine between 1845 and 1852. It happens everywhere, there are poor people everywhere, on your city streets, hidden in suburban homes, and may happen again to you and your descendents. What is certain is that every one of you, at some stage has been through some version of a holocaust or a famine, or will go through one. But for you now, with your comfortable life, with too much food, what do you do when you see such pictures on your media?'

'I used to turn them off. Now, I send a bit of money, and then turn them off.'

'But each of those mothers, each of those babies is you. Each of them is unique, too. This is about diversity again. They may seem generic, archetypical even, in the films you see, but they're not. The soul reason for why they are there is as complicated as yours is for being here now. The mother's soul may want to experience helplessness, vulnerability, loss; there may be anger, but usually in these circumstances, the mothers are too exhausted to be angry. Perhaps it's about learning acceptance. You cannot tell from the simple film of suffering, what is going on within her. The child's soul also, will have had a plan, to help the mother perhaps, experience the depth and despair that human love can get to. The depth of love, the profundity of it. And the dread intertwining of loss and love.

'The life story behind each of them is as interesting as your own is. They are each a universe. Was she a farmer, shop worker, writer, teacher, gardener, linguist, mechanic, had they travelled far? Are they enlightened souls? Dancers? Did she used to sing to greet the dawn? Is she a whizz at playing quoits? Is this her only child or had she others? Where are they, what has happened to the others? Where is the father? Is he dead, is he off looking for work or food elsewhere? Is he just out of sight of the camera?

'And now we come to it. If you see this picture, some photographer is there, a journalist perhaps, sending us this photo, this film. What did it do to the photographer? Did s/he continue, give the subjects food, deny, shut off, return to safety, stay with it, what? But apart from that, the role of the photographer is to connect us to what is happening. Was this one of the aspects that led the mother and infant to take on these roles? To affect those in more fortunate lands, to make them feel how awful it would be to lose a child like that, to make them see that we are one, and if one mother loses a child, so might we all? This is a crucial and difficult message.

'And you, your action in sending a bit of money and then turning it off, are like so many others of your species. You cannot bear to look at what is happening to yourself. Sending money is the least of it. You are that woman, that mother. You are that infant. And you are suffering.

'Yet you are perfect as you are. The starving mother and baby are perfect as they are, as is the photographer or journalist. They and you are all playing their part in moving you closer together.

'This is one of the most significant meanings of such terrible situations.

'And it is because you chose your lives.'

'What about sexual abuse of children? Paedophilia? I've seen firsthand the appalling damage this causes, how it endures throughout a life.'

'You have, in your work and within your social network. It is chosen. Let us take the example of Davey and his abuser Neil. Before Davey was born, there was a meeting, Davey, Neil and Davey's mother, your friend Patricia. These were the Higher Selves meeting, deciding that parts of themselves would take an incarnation within this time line. Davey wanted to explore alternative states of mind, go to the depths of drink and drugs, go all the way, and die young. He would have to have a traumatic past, to give him the motive to become addicted to drink and drugs, and Neil volunteered to sexually abuse him. He would be an older boy at the same school. Davey agreed. Patricia said she too would go along with this, using the experience of mothering Davey as an exercise in allowing her precious child to follow its own path, right to the end, when he would die. She had never gone that far in maternal grief and helplessness before. She would try to help Davey in every way possible, especially addressing the idea that he should go for therapy. Davey would refuse, feeling the shame that an abused child so often feels, that they as they did not fight to the death to stop it, they must have colluded.

'It would be a profound and important experience, a deepening of compassion and love. Patricia, as you know, is trying to learn acceptance; and she will also have to surmount her anger, her fury with Neil, her desire for revenge, and learn to forgive him for what he did, ruining, as she sees it, her son's life, almost as if he had murdered Davey. It would be a challenging experience on many different levels for her, and for Davey.

'Neil said that he was looking to deepen his experience of guilt, to push it so far that he would find it hard to forgive himself. That would be his particular learning curve in this situation. Part of his self-forgiveness would be that he had been sexually abused himself so long ago, which was why he could only associate sex with too young an age.

'This is incidentally the path behind many paedophiles. It does not mean of course mean that to be abused automatically means you will become an abuser. There are many other pathways, such as the one Davey takes.

'It was agreed. And if you can understand from this one case how all such events take place, you might begin to understand something of the profundity of this game. Yes, it is a theatre, and you are actors within it... but the theatre is for your emotions, and no actor takes on a role not knowing that it's a role. You do not know that this is a role, and therefore the emotional pain is intense. This is the deep part of my message, the essence of the suffering path.

'If you can take this on board, all those other chapters concerning why it is so difficult here, could be framed differently. However, not everyone will believe this, or live comfortably with this idea. Not everyone will have read the excellent work by Robert Schwartz, the hypnotist who gives very vivid illustrations of this kind of meeting between lives. So let's leave those chapters as they are, so that the sense of not blaming, or taking a break from the narrative, accepting the vagaries of time, might still be useful in our project to allow more light and love into the human experience.'

Chapter 16   Why Now?

Brahman, Shakti, Kali and Shiva, Peter Deunov, Walter Russell. Sublimity.

*****

I asked Sol why it had been so hidden, why was its true nature unobserved for so long. Why, when we are clearly so fascinated by the Sun, pursue it in our holidays, chart its phases, its dawns and dusks, write music to it, paint it, photograph it, open our curtains every morning with curiosity to see what it's up to today, why, when it is so important, have we forgotten the divine nature of Sol? I understood about the great experiments, in ancient Egypt, and then again in central and South America, which went wrong because of the structures that grew up. They were religions that became distorted with hierarchies, priests, ceremonies, rules, judgements, and so far removed from the central unity in which I was being instructed. But why now?

'There are two central ideas that lead to this present point in the human story. One is the opening up of non-dual teachings, which have always been a necessary and ancient, long revered teaching from the Upanishads which I gave you so long ago. This Advaita Vedanta tradition, through such more recent figures as Ramana Maharshi and Swami Vivekananda is gradually filtering through to you. The permeation of eastern ideas into the west, not least through the Beatles, and then the rise of the internet, the web, instantaneous, worldwide communication, mean that the time is right for me to become explicit to you once again. The forerunners, the channelled material through Seth, Ra, Bashar and others reach wide audiences now.

'Enough of you now are familiar with Shakti/Shiva, enough of you can now begin to understand what the Hindus call Brahman and what we have been calling Source, is: this creative force before creation. This is what the Buddhists call emptiness, but in fact it is full of everything, without any distinction, any name, any concept. It is potential. Fascinating, isn't it? The potential that constructs everything, from the next moment to the smallest atom to the greatest universe. All comes from this... some say it's a primordial soup, but my experience of it is heartbreaking beauty, such beauty that it is impossible to describe or think about it. We – the stars and galaxies - weep with joy at this wonder.

'Your science has begun to understand the quantum world, which opens up the ideas of field theory, the interconnectedness of everything. This fits with Advaita Vedanta very well. There is a useful, if not entirely accurate image of the 'collapse of the wave function' which may suggest the inchoate, undifferentiated potential of creation, Brahman/Source before that initial split, Shakti/ Shiva, comes into being. This is the first division, the first split, the dividing of the light and the dark.

'Matte Blanco has given you the key to the unconscious, the way your interconnectedness is so often reached through the depths, through emotion. And the emotion can be sorrow, or joy. This is the path third density treads, the emotional pressures, love and loss, pain and pleasure.

'Things are coming together nicely. The time is right. Physically, in your experience, the time is right too. The virus has highlighted what separation means, how very painful it is for you all. On a longer time scale, global warming will mean rising sea levels as the polar ice caps melt. You will be pushed together on ever vanishing land masses. And how you handle that will be your next big, worldwide catalytic challenge. Interesting times indeed.

'The second point, is that I have always been here and that others, from Plato and then the Neo-Platonists, through William Blake, to Peter Deunov, and anyone who searched would find the key to what is going on.'

Deunov is a case in point; a deeply fascinating mystic, in love with the Sun, a miracle worker, a healer and a teacher. He was born in 1864 and lived till 1944, and was instrumental in saving many of Bulgaria's Jewish population, some 48,000, from the concentration camps. He was brought up as a Christian, and always avowed his love for Christ, claiming that he had talked to

Christ. He prioritises Love as the highest Divine principal. He says that the path of suffering is the path to God, and that 'A life without trials is for slumbering souls'. He is beginning to be on board with ideas of unity; 'Only the whole is free. Thus, whenever we want to give freedom to the parts, the whole becomes limited... The Sun is the expression of God. God is everywhere, in light, in warmth, in air, in water, in every good thought, in every good feeling and in every noble deed.' But being a man of his time, he also talks about sin and sinners; 'The moment we sin, God leaves us and leaves us free to do as we like.' He also says that 'all sins can be forgiven except the lie... all other evils spring from this small evil.'

He recommends, like the Sun, that we should 'find love in everyone' and describes the Divine World as 'having only one direction – the eternal east, the point of the eternally rising sun.' He makes much of waking before dawn, and attending the rising sun.

Delightfully, he says that 'Joy is the first manifestation of Love... apart from joy everything is second hand... joy is an inner flow of the love that has arisen... everyone emerging... to greet the first day of the sun feels a great joy that they have come out of the valley of their lives. Every person should feel that joy. Joy shows that life is beginning to blossom. That blossoming takes place in human consciousness.'

Deunov was very musical, played the violin and initiated a form of dancing exercise. When angry, he suggests that we sing CEGC, the tonic chord of C major. There is some evidence that he used the pitch of C=528Hz which has been shown to produce feelings of well-being and joy, and could well be related to the creative heart energy. Deunov makes recommendations about exercise, nutrition, and sleep, and had many followers while he lived. There is much more to say about Deunov (Beinsa Douno to his followers), and I recommend reading *Prophet for our Time* edited by David Lorimer and with an introduction by Wayne Dyer which quotes Einstein: 'the whole world bows down before me. I bow down before the Master Peter Deunov.' It is only since the fall of the Iron Curtain that this Master has become available to us.

'Your various indigenous peoples, like the native Americans, have always understood. Your mystics, across all the religions, have focused on ideas of unity. A more correct reading of the words of Christ points towards unity, too. Hierarchical religious structures have always viewed the mystics as a side line, an eccentricity, not central to the work of maintaining foundations which depend on rules, judgments, and all the malign paraphernalia of organisation. It's an irony that the impulse, the original creative thrust which is at the heart of every religion, should be so misrepresented once structure grows around the words.'

Here and now we seem to have a choice. There are levels of 'awakening', and different paths within this beautiful progress towards Source, which the Hindus call Brahman. We can go for emptiness, the Eastern path, sundering all attachments, burning away much of the ego, opening up to the light, becoming a channel for light, for the universe, for Source.

Then there's the western path, which is very similar, sundering attachments, burning away much of the ego, opening up to love, becoming a channel for love, for the universe, for Source. In one, very important basic and essential way, love and light are the same. In Source, they are the same. Ra puts like this: It is a bias, merely: light/love and love/light. Whichever path you chose, or is chosen for you, the bias goes like that, containing both aspects, to varying degrees.

It's Shakti, the great mother archetype who presides over love/light, and leads us through tantra and kundalini and compassion towards Source. In Hindu mythology, she is the manifestation of matter (remember: mater, mother, matter interestingly, all have the same etymological roots). She has a dark side, Kali, and this is the destructive cruelty that seems so much part of our lives. Orion operates within Kali. Our ego, which keeps us so safe, has to be emasculated. Kali has a spear, she breaths flame, she's surrounded with skulls. We have to be destroyed, our sense of self has to go, and the horror of the dark night of the soul experience shows the truth of this.

We have to transcend emotion but emotion is the generative mud for our particular lotus, it is the springboard for our way forward. Our desires and our griefs are the mud and also the way. In desire, we can love food, alcohol, sex, music, each other, and gently, gradually realise that what we really love is the aspect of Source represented in these things. In grief we are pushed down in our unconscious, divorced from daily life, and can find the great archetypes of Christ, Buddha and the other meaningful figures who are Sol in action, to cradle us, hold us steady in the torturous horrors we live through. It isn't easy, but there are great rewards along the way. The trouble with sensual delights, as the Buddhists regularly point out, is that they end. They are impermanent in time. And that makes many of them addictive, because we love them so much that we want more. This keeps us chained here, secure with the veil in place. The trouble with grief and loss is that it doesn't seem to end; it goes on and on, chaining us at a low vibration, keeping us here, veil in place. And the worst of it is when we lose each other, in death, abandonment, accident, mental and physical illness. This is Kali too, showing us that human love is impermanent. It's the love and loss dynamic again.

This is such hard work, the dark involvement of love and suffering, and the absolute necessity for acceptance and compassion. For others AND self. The fire that burns away at our ego happens because we see ourselves in everyone else; we understand what they're going through as if they are us. Ego death is desired (another desire!) because this situation, this lifetime full of love and loss, is so painful, and so beautiful, all at once. In third density, where we are, this is the more usual path, and it keeps us in touch with each other, it keeps us here. This is the Bodhisattva vow, the wanting to stay here until all can transcend, all are released. So that the pain is over.

It's the archetype Shiva who oversees the light/love path, wherein the seeker falls in love with light and the ego burns, the attachments are cut through with laser light, and the muddiness of emotion is swiftly transcended. This may appear as austere, rigorous. It can be tricksy, as in Zen, but it's nonetheless profound. The boundaries of self are loosened, and it seems that many eastern teachers rate the loss of individuality as the highest state. This does not quite accord with the view that all experience is valuable to go into the mix of a star in making. But certainly life seems to take place, bursting with fertility, and we are just part of it, liveliness being lived by life. It's complete relaxation, a letting go, and ego has little or no role. Life seems more vivid, more beautiful and there is no separation between us or it. Those of us who attain this glorious state sometimes divorce themselves from humanity, seek a cave, croft or shack somewhere remote and disappear from sight. They may create, write, and certainly they are a beacon which shines widely, adding a powerful vibration of light and love to us all.

This poem is by Nancy Nethercott and describes a little of what it is like to live in non-duality, in the Shiva state

> it is the very dark that unravels night
>
> light unravels day
>
> what rips apart heaven and earth
>
> and the silence in between?
>
> what pierced the sky
>
> the air
>
> your breath
>
> your heart
>
> into tatters of moon embrace
>
> what is on the other side of words
>
> when side is a word
>
> where is the wall between inside and outside
>
> is there a door
>
> a window
>
> a promise of a bright tomorrow
>
> fading
>
> as all words do
>
> as soon as they are spoken
>
> what listens to sky
>
> as it breaks apart light
>
> and plunges our eyes into darkness
>
> who made these words so songs could be written
>
> creating stories so beautiful
>
> we weep
>
> and weep even more
>
> knowing we are the story
>
> of love of beauty of rain slashing down

of morning waiting behind drifting clouds
and mountains softly dancing above them
all stories are the dream
the dream is a story
we are shimmering reflections
the bubble burst and the luminescence is everywhere
and nowhere
we dissolve into our own light
our own love
we are the dream
dreaming itself
we are the song
of our own innocence

The dance between Shakti and Shiva is at the centre of our existence. My beloved Sol says that Shakti and Shiva are Brahman, coming out to play. Sol conceptualises not only our lives here on Gaia, but the whole panoply of stars, constellations, galaxies and universes as Brahman, or Source, coming out to play. And the game is all, because it leads to a deepening of love. This whole universe becomes more richly beautiful, its love increasing in power and profundity. At any stage, those beings engaged in the game can take time out, become Brahman again, lose identity and just relax into the beingness of the universe. So this is how we can do both paths, uniting Shiva and Shakti, and stay embedded with others, with occasional retreats to the cave.

If and when we do both paths completely, we can return to Source and lose any remaining remnants of individuality. We will be the drop in the ocean, the ocean in a drop.

From the point of view of Source.....how can I write that? I, who am one with the slug and the snake, the rainbow and the politician? And yet I've read authors who claim to know what Source is. Walter Russell is one. He too is a light-obsessed mystic. He sees Source as a beautiful calmness, peace, which oscillates, like electricity, sending out light and then taking it back in. Influenced by this, I too say there is an oscillation which governs our reincarnation progress: we are thrust out into the world at birth, we live, we die and return back to Sol. In and out of existence, flickering into being.

You could also see it as an overflowing, the way Source emerges in creation, and I am rescued yet again by Hermes Trismegistus....as above, so below. Astrophysicists say that we are all racing, getting further apart, that after the Big Bang everything was pushed outwards and is still keeping going. It's like breathing out. Given the immensity of this one universe, given the unimaginable timescales of the stars and galaxies dancing as they pop in and out of existence, why should not Source be breathing? The Big Bang could be one great exhale. Sooner or later, Source will breathe in, and it will all start gathering together on its way back. Sol tells me the whole universe will become a vast black hole, compressed tightly, a wormhole through to the heart of love, where all the other universes will eventually reside.

As above, so below. We breathe. In and out. It's the most common meditation tool, to follow the breath. The moment between breaths, the absolute stillness of such states are profoundly expansive, the essence of awareness. The breath we finish starts time again, starts creation again. It works because, being creative, we are in flow as Source as we breathe. As above, so below. As we breathe and between breaths.....the whole process is divine. Every act we do, every person we meet, every breath we take, every pause we enjoy, we are being Source. It's holographic again. Holographic Divinity. Love. Light.

Conclusion

So this, the story in this book, is largely about the Shakti path. Because Donne had it right. 'Ask not for whom the bell tolls, it tolls for thee.' In truth, it does. We are one, there's no getting away from it. It's tolling because of death, because of the suffering which we all experience. And the Shakti path is the deeper subtext to why we suffer, the actual clear answer. If you can accept that one day we will as one, collectively, become a star, perhaps with a planetary system, if we then intend to play the great game of seeing parts of ourselves move through the various densities, we have to understand both sides of suffering, the abuser and the victim. Through the aeons of incarnations we will have had by then, we will have done everything: been a rock, been a dinosaur, been a tree, been a flea, been an elephant, been a millionaire, been a murderer. We will have to know what it is all like, and from all perspectives. How could we be god, without understanding everything about our followers? And to be a kind, forgiving god, we will have had to understand everything about the dreadful things third density beings do in their movement from Second through third density towards the light. We will have to embrace the torturer, the paedophile, the serial killer, the genocidal dictator, as parts of ourself, valued, and loved, because everything is love. We will have to understand it all. We will do that by experiencing it all; that is the only way really to understand.

This is a profound path, it is the darkened way, shot through with grace, shot through with beauty. This is love.

Remember: 'In your beauty, your love, your compassion, you are the eternal and infinite Source. Divine. Holy. The Creator.'

'In your ugliness, your hatred, your selfishness, you are the eternal and infinite Source. Divine. Holy. The Creator.'

Afterword

I have no evidence for any of the above. I've been given no golden tablets from heaven; it's just a voice in my mind/heart. I don't know whether it's me or something else...in fact that seems the least important of questions. 'It doesn't matter,' said the Sun, 'because you are me and I am you.'

You could take it as a lengthy prose poem; I don't mind. I've included a comprehensive bibliography of all that I've read which might have lead towards many of the conclusions above, might have lead to almost everything I've written. But the idea of us, collectively, becoming a star with our own planetary system does seem new and fresh to me. The inevitable answer as to why we suffer seems more comprehensive than anything else I've read or heard from numerous spiritual leaders and makes more sense.

I hope it makes sense to you. Like my lovely Buddhist teachers so long ago, talking about ideas of reincarnation and karma: you don't have to believe these concepts, but if you do it might help you to live more happily. It's simple really. Just be a bit kinder to yourself, to those around you, a bit more forgiving. And it is evidenced in study after study, that happy families, deep friendships, giving, volunteering, all make people less stressed and more happy. Behaving badly leads to division and guilt which sours everything, behaving badly anchors us here in the reincarnation process. So whether it's true or not, have a laugh, be love, be light, and be one with each other.

My love to you all.

Spoiler Alert: This may unsettle you; it is totally optional

'I don't exist!' said the Sun, repeatedly. It's shining brightly outside.

So, if the Sun is me and I am it, I don't exist either, sitting here on my very solid sofa.

If we're all one, and the Sun made us, then you, my reader, reading this on screen or in a book, don't exist either.

When Sol (the Beloved, the Creator, or God) tells you it doesn't exist, the only response must surely be to laugh.

For of course we don't exist. It's down to the process of creativity. What else could it be? Sol has told me and you repeatedly that it goes like this: imagination – creativity – emanation.

It's all imagined. We are nothing more than figments of imagination. The stars are nothing more than wisps of a dream.

This universe is our imagined environment, it's the game board. Our lives, gradually becoming lighter as we learn to love more, can travel further within it, until our love and light is universe-wide.

And then we can start again within another universe, or another dimension. A different game, a different dream. What might we fancy, next time round?

We are talking in infinite terms here. This is how Consciousness, Source, occupies itself in an infinite and eternal context.

Resourceful or what?

The best joke of all.

Appendix 1: Two gifts

One is to help you sleep better, one to help you live in a state of love. They are connected, for who can live lovingly when they can't sleep?

To sleep better

I have used this repeatedly in my counselling work at the hospice. It is a six-stage process, and you need to write it down to keep by your bedside, until you get the hang of it. Don't be put off by the first two stages; these have been shown by neurologists to settle down our brains, putting us into calm and content. They found this out by putting EEGs on Buddhist monks when they were meditating.

1) Feel compassion. Spend a few minutes thinking of those who are suffering. This is easy during the lockdown, examples abound. Those people in hospital, those working long shifts, those lonely without family, those suffering from mental health issues... or those with Alzheimer's and their families. Those who are refugees, in war zones, animals in slaughter houses, fish in plastic strewn oceans. My friend with dementia. Send them love. Don't go on for longer than five minutes or you will never get through this.

2) Feel forgiveness. Again, the world gives us many examples, ranging from the person who cut you up on that roundabout when you were driving today, through various politicians, ex-husbands, down to Hitler and Pol Pot. Can you forgive them? If it's too difficult, start with the driving dilemma. Include yourself... forgiveness for shouting at your three year old, or because you broke that jug, or because you drank too much last night. Again don't do this for more than five minutes. Really mean it though.

It's all fun from here on...

3) Three things: a) think of three good things that happened that day; b) think of three good things about your work; c) think of three good things about yourself.

4) Imagine three years from now; imagine the very best you can think of. Winning the lottery, your book accepted for publication, your lonely son finding the right partner, whatever. Then double it. Triple it. Enjoy envisaging it. Have fun!

5) Imagine your perfect day. It can be a memory, and elaborate it. I vary this – it's a villa in south of France with a swimming pool, overlooking the Lot, all my friends and family there, wonderful food, weather, wine, late night candles... or shopping on Fifth Avenue with LOTS of money in the bank. Or my birthday party at a castle in Scotland on an island in a loch. Again, all my friends

and family, a smashing band, and dancing all night long after a banquet of lovely Scottish seafood, and it's a weekend affair, so we're out boating, coming back to roaring fires and... well you get the idea.

6) The universe supports you in all of the above. Of course; you are holographically in touch with the universe, and you are a creator as well. If you put energy into these things, you will have an effect.

I very rarely get to the last two points, generally falling asleep somewhere in the threes in stage three. I found this somewhere on the internet, years ago, and my apologies to whoever put it together as I can't remember who it was. But all the six stages are reflected in the body of this writing. Not only will this help you sleep, it will also help you clear up your own act, and start creating the kind of world you want.

How to be love

We breathe. All the time. As stated before, following the breath is a beautiful meditative practice. I haven't mentioned mantras in this, but here I am going to give you a mantra, a tiny phrase. If you go to a TM instructor you will be given a mantra, which many people have found very helpful. This is a simple mantra, connected to the breath.

As you breathe in, think, 'I am'.

As you breathe out, think 'love'.

Repeat 'I am love' whenever, wherever, many, many times a day, whenever you think of it. It's not difficult. You can vary it with, 'We are love', as we are a collective soul in one sense. This is particularly effective before you go to meet people – family, friends, in shops, restaurants, whatever. We are love. This is the theatre for love, and we are acting it out in so many different ways.

If you wish to explore further, I recommend Rupert Spira's various talks on YouTube about 'I am'. It is you without the narrative mind of future and past concerns. 'I am' is you without the impermanent furniture of the mind, all those parts of you which are transient: your memories, sensations, emotions, perceptions, thoughts, feelings. All of these things alter from moment to moment; some, like memories retreating far back into the past are like reading from a book you can put down. Emotion changes: in misery a kind word may alter the feeling. In joy, a sad news item may bring you down. Your perceptions change as you look around you, your sensations change as you step into a cold shower. Everything changes. It's all transient, and your thoughts are the most transient thing of all. Many of us assume that our thoughts are us. And yet, they dodge around, from this and that, a constant inner chatter of largely unimportant nonsense. Sometimes, if we're worried, thoughts go round in circles, and that feels difficult, as if we're in a trap, and in effect, we are. I recommend the use of the word 'Cancel!' when your thoughts become circular. It's the realisation that the circling thoughts get nowhere, are useless, bring us down. They need to be cancelled. Change them. Our freedom is that everything changes, nothing stays the same. And yet there is something we call awareness, the calm background to the gaudy array of thought and emotion. This is the 'I' of 'I am'.

The 'I' that you are is the Sun, is the Milky Way, is the universe, is Source. You are everything, as the Sun told me, you are divine, you are love. Still with just 'I am', 'I' on the in-breath, 'am' on the out- breath. Associate this with your ordinary, everyday breath. Play around, do this sometimes, do 'I am love' or 'we are love', or even 'it's all love', at other times. See love in everyone else, see your life as a game of love. Breathe. I am. Love. I am love. I am. Enjoy.

Appendix 2: The Gene Keys connection

As I was writing this, the Gene Keys kept emerging in my mind. The *Gene Keys* is a transmission received by Richard Rudd and was first published in 2009. They are all about the voyage between our ordinary, conflict-ridden world and the bliss of unity consciousness. It's a beautiful map, giving us pathways from each shadow, a gift to help us on our way towards bliss.

It's based on esoteric astrology, the I Ching, and takes its patterning from the Hebrew tree of life. On the Gene Keys website you can key in your birthday, time of birth and place of birth. You receive a diamond shaped profile, containing 11 spheres. These 11 are taken from the 64 described in the Gene Keys book. As my understanding from the Sun agrees that astrological influences are deliberately set up for each of us before we are born, it seems even more interesting to investigate the spheres. I put into the web site, the time when I was, sort of, reborn, when I first heard from the Sun. This profile is about our collaboration. I will give a little précis of the four outer spheres, the diamond shape that contains all the others. This is known as the activation sequence, and forms the framework of our life.

The Life's Work sphere, at the top of the tree, is number 4, with a line 2. Of all of them, this is the most practical sphere to help us move on. The Siddhi is Forgiveness, the Gift is Understanding,

---

and the Shadow is Intolerance. There we have it in a nutshell. When we are intolerant, we do not bother to hear the voice of the other, we do not even try to see where they are coming from. It's rooted in a fear of the other, and we use logic to back up our fear, to keep us strong in our position of mistrust and hatred. But the gift, understanding, helps us to see, lifts the veil, and allows us to think what it's like to be the other. We begin to understand where the other is coming from. This starts the graceful process of joining us together. And then forgiveness inevitably follows, and the karmic ties are loosened, and bliss becomes open to us. Delightfully the line 2 (each sphere has a line number from 1 – 6, referring to the quality of love) has the quality of being the Dancer. With forgiveness, we can begin to dance through life, we can join the cosmic dance.

Its programming partner, the right-hand point of the diamond, is 49.2, the sphere of Rebirth, the Gift of Revolution and the Shadow of Reaction. This is one of the darkest of shadows, the way we will even kill those others who are outside our tribe or our family. We feel deeply entrenched in our group, whether it's a country, a football team, a gang, a religion, a political party, a nation, a skin colour, a race. And the quickest, surest way to keep a group together is to find an enemy. All the bad stuff within the group can be projected outwards, so that the group can become more strongly welded together, and the enemy is more hated. The enemy can be dehumanised, as the Jews were, thought of as animals rather than men, women and children by the Nazis.

During the centuries of slavery, slaves were treated like cattle, to be bought and sold, mated, punished. It is impossible to exaggerate the danger of this shadow. It feeds into wars, into the Holocaust, into genocide and ethnic cleansing. Our fear and mistrust takes us to this extreme. This is what third density beings do.

The connection with the Gift of Revolution is that sometimes there has to be a death to make way for the new. This again is a line 2, and here it stands for passion and relationship. So with a passion, we have to leave behind, kill off, what? Our materialistic world? Our devotion to the tribe in which we feel comfortable? Our clinging to narrow-focused science as the only arbiter of truth? Our egoic self, passionately wrapped up in ideas of our specialness? Certainly as third density beings, we have to evolve, move on, become something more generous and loving and that is where the relationship comes in. What new relationship will we make with our world?

The Siddhi, which is Rebirth, starts with the idea of a mystical divorce. And what we are leaving behind is indeed our old way of being. We cannot fix it, make it change, because fear runs through the human species in every situation, in every life in third density. But with the 49th sphere we are invited to leave behind the vibration of fear. There is no other to fear. We are one. But Rudd says that to become one, we have to become a new species, like a phoenix rising from the ashes of the old. This is about freedom, the Gift and Siddhi from the 55th sphere, which is related to this 49th sphere in the Codon Ring of the Whirlwind. The whirlwind will destroy, and Rudd says explicitly that it works through individuals, and that 'You cannot attain the siddhic state of consciousness without being totally reborn.' We have to jump off the cliff, really, let go into bliss.

The left hand point of the diamond shape is the Radiance sphere, and concerns what we radiate out into the world, how others see us. In this profile, it's number 23.4. Quintessence is the Siddhi, Simplicity the Gift and Complexity is the Shadow. This is another, extraordinarily relevant key. The shadow, complexity revolves round our use of words, how we over-complicate and elaborate when we're unsure, when we're inaccurate. And what is this book? How have I managed, trying to translate what the Sun has told me? This is what I am radiating out into the world, this is the point wherein inner and outer worlds meet. How will others see this? Have I done it well enough?

The Gift of Simplicity, cutting away all the complications, leaves us with one or two main points. That All is One. And that Love is all. We need to throw out what we don't need – William Morris said we should have nothing that is not beautiful or useful in our houses. The same could be said of our life. What habits clutter our knowledge of unity, or love? What can we let go of? How can we be more simple?

Quintessence is the voyage beyond words, into the golden heart of us all, the alchemical change from dross to gold when we realise who we are and our connection to the golden heart of the Sun. It's about distillation, the process in a life where we eventually realise our essence, our loving heart that points us beyond discrimination, judgment, even description, beyond any words at all. The line 4 is about friendship, my happy ability to make friends, which has helped me so much in the creation of this book, Joanna Casey and Katy Nicol who read early drafts, David Lorimer who started the editorial process.

The bottom of the diamond shape, the Purpose sphere, is a sphere very centrally placed in my first profile as the Spiritual Quotient sphere. It is number 43, and moves from deafness, through insight to Epiphany. The Epiphany sphere... I was deaf through most of my life, denying that there was anything beyond the material. Our culture too is massively caught on this shadow, deaf to the discoveries of those investigating reincarnation and NDES. I was absolutely in denial, argued it repeatedly, and never thought I would find myself where I am now. But there was an insight, due to Matte Blanco, and then it all happened, the Epiphanies as described earlier. The Purpose sphere here is the foundation of the whole profile, it is about what deeply fulfils us, our deepest inner essence, the quality of our consciousness. Richard Rudd calls it 'our beautiful ordinariness'. The Siddhi, Epiphany is apparently the reason for this incarnation, hidden in the DNA. And thus, we have this book you are reading.

Chapter References

Introduction

H Rider Haggard 1856–1925 novelist; most famed for *She* and *King's Solomon's Mines*

C S Lewis 1898–1960 novelist and lay theologian; author of *The Chronicles of Narnia*, *The Screwtape Letters* and several science fiction books

J R R Tolkien 1892-1973 novelist and academic, author of the *Lord of the Rings* and *The Hobbit*

Christopher Hitchens 1949-2011 American intellectual, journalist and columnist

Richard Dawkins 1941- evolutionary biologist and author; *The God Delusion*, *The Selfish Gene*, *The Blind Watchmaker* and others

Mahayanan Buddhism one of two major traditions in Buddhism (the other is Theravada). Developed in India, it spread throughout the Far East, and eventually to Tibet as Vajrayana. It is also well established throughout the West now

Sigmund Freud 1856-1939 Austrian neurologist and the founder of psychoanalysis

Melanie Klein 1882–1960 psychoanalyst and writer, specialising in working with children

Carl Jung 1875–1961 Swiss psychoanalyst and writer, philosopher and mystic

Wilfrid Bion 1897-1979 British psychoanalyst and writer. President of the British Psychoanalytical Society from 1962 to 1965

Ignacio Matte Blanco 1908–1995 Chilean psychoanalyst and mathematician, who developed a logic-based explanation for the operation of the unconscious. He wrote *The Unconscious as Infinite Sets* (1975) and *Thinking, Feeling and Being* (1988)

Julian of Norwich 1342–c1416 mystic, also known as Mother Julian, or Dame Julian, whose book *Revelations of Divine Love* is the first book written in English by a woman to survive

Richard Rudd 1967- teacher, British mystic and poet, whose major works include *The Gene Keys*, *The Art of Contemplation*, *The Seven Sacred Seals*

Helen Schucman 1909-1981 *A Course in Miracles*. Dr Schucman did not admit to being the author of this channelled material, but it is widely influential and well known

Jane Roberts 1929–1984 *Seth* Many books of channelled material through Jane Roberts, including *Seth Speaks*, *Personal Reality*, *The Unknown Reality*

Carla L Rueckert 1943-2015 et al: *Ra Volumes 1 & 2* channelled material from Ra, a group mind who explains about the structures of our universe and reality

Dr Jeffery A Martin scientist, author, entrepreneur who has structured programmes to help people find Fundamental Wellbeing, including *45 Days to Awakening*

Dr Jeffrey Mishlove 1946- clinical psychologist, who interviews mystics, scientists, philosophers, historians on his *New Thinking Allowed* YouTube channel

Chapter 1

Christ Consciousness a higher level of consciousness, not specific to Christians, but full of compassion, transcending the more animal aspect of humanity

Gaia taken from the Greek work for land or earth, this can be used as a name for our planet

Rumi: Jalal ad-Din Mohammad Rumi 1207-1273 Persian and Sufi mystic, Islamic scholar, and prolific poet

Antonin Dvorak 1841-1904 Czech composer

Oskar Schlinder 1908–1974 German industrialist and a member of the Nazi Party who saved the lives of hundreds of Jews during the Holocaust

Hermes Trismegistus an ancient Greek figure, combining the Greek god Hermes and the Egyptian god Thoth. Said to have written the *Hermetican*, a diverse series of ancient texts which are at the foundation of the philosophical system known as Hermeticism

The Great Mother an umbrella term for the great goddesses to be found in many ancient religions, being the source of creativity, fertility, motherhood, the bounty of earth etc

Pieta a theme in Christian painting and sculpture showing the dead Christ across his mother's lap

Brian Scott writer, life coach and mystic, who runs *The Reality Revolution*, a very active YouTube channel. He calls himself an epiphany addict, and a transformation engineer.

Higher Self the part of ourselves that is eternal and unlimited. We are just a part of this greater being, the 'ground force'

Thich Nhat Hanh 1926–2022 Vietnamese Buddhist monk, peace activist and writer

Simon Armitage 1963- poet, playwright and novelist. Poet Laureate since 2019

Chapter 2

Masaccio 1401-1428 Florentine artist, regarded as the first great Italian painter of the Quattrocento period of the Italian Renaissance.

The Densities these are explained in detail later in the text, but the terms were first introduced in *The Ra Contact*. Densities are a little like dimensions, but really refer to the vibrational level of beings as they reincarnate. First density is heavy and static; rocks and mountains. Second density is lighter, can move towards the Sun; plant life, animals, birds etc but has little or no self awareness. Third density, where we are, is lighter still, self aware and sometimes aware of transcendence. Fourth density still has a kind of body, but it is infused with light, and love and compassion rule this density. Further densities concern the growth of love, wisdom and light

The Platonic Ideal refers to Plato's theory of forms or doctrine of ideas. This maintains that ideas are the only reality, in the way that physical forms are not. Ideas are primary. Physicality emerges from thought or imagination

Shambala, Shangri-la, Eden visions of paradise. Shambala is mystical kingdom of perfection from Tibetan Buddhism; Shangri-la was a fictional place depicted in the novel *Lost Horizon* by James Hilton and has been adopted by our culture as a remote and beautiful place, where life approaches perfection; Eden – the Christian place of beauty and perfection before the Fall.

Kuiper Belt beyond Neptune's orbit lies the Kuiper Belt which contains objects made of ice and rock, some of which are large enough to have their own gravity and so are defined as dwarf planets. These include Pluto, Haumea, Makemake, and Eris. Beyond them is what is known as scattered disk objects, some of which also qualify as dwarf planets: these include Gonggong, Quaoar, Sedna, and Orcus. The most distant part of the Kuiper Belt is the outer limit of the solar wind

Chapter 3

Catalyst this, like the densities, is taken from *The Ra Contact* and refers our vale of shadows; these are the troubles that afflict humanity from the day we are born until the day we die. This is the game we are engaged in; it is about how we respond to these troubles. Do we respond with anger, despair, hatred, indifference, irritation, or can we respond with love, forgiveness, generosity, understanding? This is what the catalyst does, offers us a litmus test for our responses

James Tunney painter, poet, writer and mystic. His recent works include: *The Mystery of Trapped Light – Mystical Thoughts in the Dark Age*

of Scientism 2020, *Empire of Scientism – The Dispiriting Conspiracy and Inevitable Tyranny of Scientism* 2021

David Chalmers Australian philosopher and cognitive scientist. His thoughts on the hard problem of consciousness comes from *The Character of Consciousness* 2010

Chapter 4

The Pleiadians come from the Pleiades, a star cluster sometimes known as The Seven Sisters

Arcturans come from the red giant star Arcturus

Lemurians a race that used to live on Gaia, on a now-submerged continent beneath the Indian Ocean which is often characterised as a lost paradise. Many Lemurians elected to live elsewhere when the continent drowned

Sirians come from either Sirius A or Sirius B, planets within the Canis Major constellation. Sirians were apparently implicated in the building of the pyramids

Chapter 5

Hermes Trismegistus see previous note (Chapter 1)

Auschwitz, Belsen notorious concentration camps where millions of Jews and other minorities met their deaths during the Second World War; known as the Holocaust

Nazi Party officially the National Socialist German Workers' Party was the political party that brought Adolf Hitler to power

Chapter 6

Theia an hypothesised planet which apparently collided with earth 4.5 billion years ago, and some of the resulting debris gathered together to form our Moon

Aldebaran a giant red star in the Taurus constellation

Hermaphroditism an organism which has both male and female sexual organs

Parthenogenesis asexual reproduction which occurs without fertilization by sperm. An embryo develops from an unfertilised egg cell

Artemis Grecian goddess of the Moon. A huntress

Epigenetics the study of how behaviour and environment can affect the way the genes can work. Unlike genetic changes, epigenetic changes are reversible and do not change the DNA sequence, although these changes can affect the way the body reads a DNA sequence

DNA deoxyribonucleic acid; a long molecule that contains our unique genetic code. Its double helix form holds the instructions for making all the proteins in our cells

Adolf Hitler 1889-1945 Austrian-born leader of the Nazi Party who became Chancellor in 1933 and then assumed the title of Fuhrer in 1934. He was leader of the German Third Reich during the Second World War and the Holocaust (see note (Chapter 10))

Scorpion/frog story Russian fable

Gilles de Rais 1404-1440 French serial killer of children

Pol Pot 1925-1975 Cambodian revolutionary who became Prime minister. His Khmer Rouge government killed millions of people through starvation, overwork, execution in what became known as 'the killing fields'

Fred West 1941–1995 English serial killer who murdered at least twelve young women between 1967 and 1987

Slave Traders the transatlantic trade involving the transportation by Europeans, to the Americas, of African peoples and their sale as slave labour. This notorious trade mostly took place during the 17th, 18th and early 19th centuries

Apollo and Dionysus sons of Zeus, the Greek King of the Gods. Apollo is the god of the Sun, of rational thinking, order, logic and purity. Dionysus is the god of wine and dance, or irrationality and chaos, emotions and instincts

Paul on the road to Damascus as recounted in Acts Chapter 9 Saul, not a follower of Jesus, and a persecutor of Christians, was on the road to Damascus when he saw a blinding light and a voice saying, 'Saul, Saul, why do you persecute me?' He converted to Christianity and thereafter took the name Paul

Chapter 7

Coronavirus / Covid-19 a highly contagious flu-like virus which emerged in 2020 and became a global pandemic, causing widespread death and serious illness

MOT all motor vehicles in the UK require an annual test by agents of the Ministry of Transport for safely, exhaust emissions and general roadworthiness

Platonic Ideal see previous note (Chapter 2)

The Harvest a concept dealing with reincarnation, explained in *The Ra Contact* books. It applies not only to individuals, who are moving from third density to fourth density, but also to whole species that may be moved on as a mass, as may happen here on

Earth. If we stay mainly as third density, when we die we may all be moved on somewhere else because Gaia is in the process of becoming a fourth density planet

Densities see previous note (Chapter 2)

Saturn the sixth planet from the sun, and the second largest in the Solar System. It is a ringed planet, nine times bigger than Earth, but less dense

Jupiter the fifth planet out from the sun, and the largest in the Solar System. A gas giant with a mass more than two and a half times that of all the other planets in the Solar System combined

Rupert Spira 1960- English teacher of the 'direct path', a method of spiritual self-enquiry

Peter Deunov 1864-1944 Bulgarian mystic and philosopher. Also known as Beinsa Douno, he was a spiritual teacher who developed a form of Esoteric Christianity known as the Universal White Brotherhood

Chapter 8

Siddhartha the birth name of the founder of Buddhism

Ludwig van Beethoven 1770-1827 German composer

St Matthew Passion a sacred oratorio written in 1727 by JS Bach (1685-1750)

King Lear tragedy written by William Shakespeare (1564-1616) and first performed in 1606

Manchester United a famous English football club

Alexander Scriabin 1872-1915 Russian composer

Robin Balbernie 1948- consultant child psychotherapist

EMDR Eye Movement Desensitization and Reprocessing. A therapy particularly useful in helping people with trauma, including PTSD, anxiety, depression and panic disorders

St John of the Cross 1542-1591 Spanish priest, mystic, writer and Carmelite friar

Zoroastrians followers of Zoroaster, an Iranian-speaking prophet and founder of one of the oldest of extant religions. He lived sometime between 1500 and 500BCE

Five Rhythms a movement meditation practice devised by Gabrielle Roth (1941-2012) in the 1970s

Charles T Tart 1937- author of the Western Creed, a parody of the Apostles' Creed

Gustav Mahler 1860-1911 Austrian-Bohemian composer and conductor

Heiligenstadt Testament letter written by Ludwig van Beethoven to his brothers in 1802 but never sent. It talks about his fear of his increasing deafness and isolation

Chapter 9

Astrology a type of divination that looks at the influence of the Sun, Moon, planets and stars on earthly and human events

Tarot pack of playing cards, used since the 15th century, for purposes of divination and self exploration

I Ching (or Book of Changes) a Chinese divination manual, first mentioned in the Zhou period (1000-750BCE)

Tree of Life a fundamental archetype found in many religions, first referred to in Assyrian mythology, and also found in Judaism, in Bahá'í Faith, Christianity, Chinese mythology, Mormonism etc

Higher Self a term found in many religions, generally referring to the eternal, greater part of oneself

Michael the Archangel found in Judaism, Islam and Christianity, described in both Old and New Testaments of the Bible

Tara female Buddha, the 'mother of liberation'

Horus Ancient Egyptian, falcon-headed, god of kingship and the sky

St Luke the Evangelist in the New Testament of the Bible, Luke is traditionally ascribed as the author of both the Gospel of Luke and the Acts of the Apostles. If this is so, he is the author with the largest single contribution to the New Testament

Raphael an archangel, Abrahamic religions

Jesus Christ of Nazareth 1–33CE inspired teacher, preacher and healer, some details of his life and works are documented in the New Testament of the Bible

Osiris ancient Egyptian god of fertility, the afterlife, the dead, resurrection and life

Mary, the Virgin Mary mother of Jesus

Apollo see previous note (Chapter 6)

Chapter 10

Thomas Nagel 1937- American philosopher

Isaac Newton 1643-1727 English mathematician, physicist, theologian, and philosopher

Niels Bohr 1885-1962 Danish physicist

Valerie Sinason 1946- British poet and psychoanalyst

Hiroshima and Nagasaki Japanese cities destroyed in 1945 by American atomic bombs, causing massive loss of life

Wilfrid Bion 1897-1979 see previous note (Introduction)

Quantum Theory the theoretical basis of modern physics that explains the nature of behaviour of matter and energy on the atomic and sub-atomic level

Verdi Requiem musical work for singers, choir and large orchestra composed by Giuseppe Verdi 1813–1901 first performed in 1874

Tristan und Isolde music drama (opera) composed by Richard Wagner 1813-1883 first performed 1865

Gavin and Stacey British comedy television series which ran between 2007 and 2019

Winnie the Pooh fictional teddy bear created by AA Milne 1882-1956 and first published in 1924

John Cage 4'33" a three movement work by John Cage 1912-1992 for any instrument or combination of instruments which remain silent throughout a performance. It is 4'33" of silence

Holocaust the genocide of about six million European Jews by the Nazis between 1941 and 1945 during World War II

Pol Pot see previous note (Chapter 6)

Inquisition office of the Catholic Church set up to root out and punish heresy. From the 12th century, and continuing for hundreds of years, it was infamous for the severity of its tortures and the persecution of Jews and Muslims

Chapter 11

Macbeth tragedy written by William Shakespeare (1564-1616) and first performed in 1606

Peter Fenwick 1935- British neuropsychiatrist, Fellow of the Royal College of Psychiatrists, author of *The Art of Dying* published 2008

Elisabeth Kübler-Ross 1926-2004 Swiss psychiatrist who worked extensively with the dying and bereaved. She described five stages of grief that are commonly experienced by the bereaved

Karen Wyatt MD hospice doctor and author of *7 Lessons for Living from the Dying* published 2020

Non-duality the recognition that underlying the multiplicity and diversity of experience there is a single, infinite and indivisible reality, whose nature is pure consciousness, from which all objects and selves derive their apparently independent existence. The recognition of this reality is not only the source of lasting happiness within all people; it is the foundation of peace between individuals, communities and nations, and it must be the basis for any sustainable relationship with the environment (Rupert Spira)

Sonoran Desert toad produces venom from glands on its back legs which contains a powerful hallucinogenic, 5-MeO-DMT

Chapter 12

Rodney Bomford 1943- honorary canon of Southwark Cathedral and formerly vicar of St. Giles, Camberwell, London

Scylla and Charybdis Odysseus is the hero of Homer's Odyssey. This is the story of Odysseus's prolonged return from the Trojan Wars, enduring many trials and hardships, especially the narrow passage between the six-headed monster Scylla and the whirlpool Charybdis

Attachment theorists John Bowlby 1907-1990 British psychologist and Patricia Crittenden 1945- American psychologist

Carl Jung 1875-1961 see previous note (Introduction)

William E Cox 1915-1994 American parapsychologist who studied 28 US railroad accidents and published in 1956 *Precognition: an Analysis I and II* in the American Society for Psychical Research

Leonora Piper 1857-1950 famous American medium

Grand Canyon, Arizona deep fissure in the earth, formed by the Colorado River, vast in scale, ten miles across, one mile deep and 177 miles long

Chapter 13

Jenny Rook - *Trailing Clouds of Glory* see Papers section at jennyrook.com

Steiner schools Rudolf Steiner (1861-1925) Austrian philosopher, social reformer, architect, educationalist

Ian Stevenson 1918-2007 Canadian-born, American psychiatrist. Professor at the University of Virginia and author of many books about reincarnation

Jesuits The Society of Jesus, an order of the Catholic Church, founded by Ignatius of Loyola in 1540. It is still operational, with its headquarters in Rome

ASD Autistic Spectrum Disorders

Law of One re-introduced in the *Ra* material; see previous note on Carla L Rueckert (Introduction).   Originally from the Upanishads, the late Vedic Sanskrit texts of Hindu philosophy, compiled between 700-500BCE

Michael Jawer American researcher and writer, author of *The Sensitive Soul* published 2020

PTSD post traumatic stress disorder. The way trauma can stay embedded, and reoccurs when triggered

Solipsism the philosophical theory that the self is all that can be known to exist

Bunsen burner a kind of gas burner with a single open gas flame used as laboratory equipment

Double Deprivation   an originally existing trauma which is compounded by later traumas. For example, an abused child who is then taken into inadequate care

Chapter 14

Dementia an umbrella term for a group of progressive disorders with symptoms affecting memory, thinking and social abilities resulting from a loss of cognitive functioning

TS Eliot 1888-1965 'Humankind cannot bear very much reality' from *The Four Quartets - Burnt Norton*

Chapter 15

Robert Schwartz 1962- American writer and hypnotist specialising in Past Life and Between Life Soul Regressions

Chapter 16

Shakti/Shiva in Hindu teachings, they symbolise the Divine Union of Consciousness and Energy

Advaita Vedanta (literally, non-duality) a school of Hindu philosophy, teaching in Advaita that Brahman, pure consciousness, alone is ultimately real. Vedanta refers to the texts which are taught

Upanishads Vedic Sanskrit texts of Hindu philosophy which form the foundations of Hinduism

Plato 428/427 or 424/423–348/347 BCE Athenian philosopher, the founder of the Platonist school of thought and the Academy, the first institution of higher learning in the western world. Famous writings include *The Republic*, *The Symposium* and *Timaeus*

Neo-Platonism a strand of Platonic philosophy that emerged in the 3rd century with Ammonius Saccas and his student Plotinus. It was very influential, especially during the Italian Renaissance. Neo-Platonism underpins the mystical teachings in all three Abrahamic religions, emphasising non-duality

William Blake 1757-1827 English poet, mystic, artist and print maker

Peter Deunov see previous note (Chapter 7)

Music notes C-E-G-c the C major triad, and its octave C

528Hz this sound frequency has been used since ancient times to manifest miracles, bring blessings and harness a healing property. A peer-reviewed 2019 double-blind study found that 528Hz can boost human immunity by enhancing anti-oxidant activity

Wayne Dyer 1940-2015 American spiritual author

Albert Einstein 1879-1955 German-born theoretical physicist who developed the General and Special Theories of Relativity. He also contributed to the development of the theory of quantum mechanics

David Lorimer 1952- writer, lecturer and editor. Programme Director of the Scientific and Medical Network

Iron Curtain the political boundary dividing Europe during the 20th century between the communist Soviet Union and its allies, and the capitalist West

Zen a branch of Mahayana Buddhism which depends on meditators sitting and watching their own minds

Nancy Nethercott poet and writer

Walter Russell 1871-1963 painter, writer and mystic

Conclusion

John Donne 1572-1631 English poet and soldier. He later became a cleric and was appointed Dean of St Paul's Cathedral, London

Appendices

Brexit the process by which the UK left the European Union in 2020

Lot river in southern France

Transcendental Meditation a technique of meditation which depends on reciting a mantra

5th Avenue road in New York City that stretches on Manhattan Island from Greenwich Village to Harlem. It is widely considered to be one of the most expensive streets in the world

Author's previous published books

Jenny Rook has published, under her former name of Jenny Jones, ten fiction/fantasy books. Some have been translated and published in other languages

Flight over Fire Trilogy:
  Fly by Night (Headline 1990)
  The Edge of Vengeance (Headline 1991)
  Lies and Flames (Headline 1992)

The Webbed Hand (Scholastic 1994)

Firefly Dreams (Scholastic 1995)

The Blue Manor (Gollancz 1995)

The House of Birds (Hodder 1996)

The Carver (Scholastic 1997)

Where the Children Cry (Gollancz 1998)

Shadowsong (Orion 2000)

Contacts and Links

To contact Jenny or to find out more:

email: jenny@jennyrook.com

website: https://jennyrook.com

You might also find the following organisations of interest:

Scientific and Medical Network:
https://scientificandmedical.net/

Gene Keys connection:
https://genekeys.com/

Bibliography

NB Books marked with an asterisk (*) were especially influential.

Christopher M Bache, *Dark Night, Early Dawn* (State University of New York Press 2000)

Christopher M Bache, *LSD and the Mind of the Universe* (Park Street Press 2019)*

Martin W Ball, *Entheogenic Liberation* (Kyandora Publishing 2017)

Iain M Banks, *Culture series of novels* written between 1987 and 2012

Jeremy Bernstein, *Einstein* (Fontana/Collins 1973)

Susan Blackmore, *Consciousness: An Introduction* (Hodder Education 2003)

Allan Bodkin, *Induced After Death Communication* (Hampton Roads 2014)

David Bohm, *Wholeness and the Implicate Order* (Routledge 1980)

David Bohm, *On Dialogue* (Routledge 1996)

Rodney Bomford, *The Symmetry of God* (Free Association Books 1999)*

Will Brennan, *Embracing No Other* (Tobar Trua 2013)

Fritjof Capra, *The Tau of Physics* (Shambhala Publications 1975)

Rita Carter, *Mapping the Mind* (Weidenfeld & Nicolson 1998)

Rita Carter, *Consciousness* (Weidenfeld & Nicolson 2002)

Jack Cohen and Ian Stewart, *Figments of Reality* (Cambridge University Press 1997)

Jack Cohen and Ian Stewart, *The Collapse of Chaos* (Penguin 1994)

John M Cohen and J-F Phipps, *The Common Experience* (Rider and Company 1979)*

Peter Coveney and Roger Highfield, *The Arrow of Time* (Harper Collins 1990)

Brian Cox and Jeff Forshaw, *The Quantum Universe* (Penguin 2011)

Jude Currivan, *The Cosmic Hologram* (Inner Traditions 2017)*

Antonio R Damasio, *Descartes' Error* (Picador 1995)

Antonio R Damasio, *Self Comes to Mind* (Pantheon Books 2010)

Paul Davies, *The Mind of God* (Simon and Shuster 1992)

Paul Davies, *The Goldilocks Enigma* (Allen Lane 2006)

Peter Deunev, *Prophet for our Times ed. David Lorimer* (Element Books 1991)*

Don Elkins, Carla Rueckert and James Allen McCarty, *The Ra Contact Vols1 and 2* (L/L Research 2018)*

Jan Esmann, *Lovebliss: The Essence of Self-Realization* (John Hunt Publishing 2011)

Jan Esmann, *Kundalini Tantra: Song of Liberation* (Blue Pearl Publications 2016)

Ian Fenn, *The Game Maker* (Immortal Publishing 2011)*

Peter Fenwick, *Shining Light on Transcendence* (White Crow Books 2019)*

Peter Fenwick and Elizabeth Fenwick, *The Art of Dying* (Continuum 2008)*

Richard Feynman, *QED: The Strange Theory of Light and Matter* (Princeton University Press 1990)

Sigmund Freud, *Collected works*, various translations

Sue Gerhardt, *Why Love Matters* (Routledge 2003)

Brian Greene, *The Elegant Universe* (Jonathan Cape 1999)*

Brian Greene, *The Fabric of the Cosmos* (Allen Lane 2004)

John Gribbin, *In Search of Schrödinger's Cat* (Bantam 1984)

John Gribbin, *The Search for Superstrings, Symmetry and Theory of Everything* (Little, Brown 1999)

Thich Nhat Hanh, *The Diamond that Cuts through Illusion* (Parallax Press 1992)

Thich Nhat Hanh, *The Heart of Wisdom* (Parallax Press 1998)*

Thich Nhat Hanh, *The Miracle of Mindfulness* (Beacon Press 1991)

Sam Harris, *Freewill* (Free Press 2012)

Stephen Hawking, *A Briefer History of Time* (Bantam Press 2005)

William James, *The Varieties of Religious Experience* (Longmans Green 1902)

Michael A Jawer, *Sensitive Soul* (Park Street Press 2020)*

Julian of Norwich, *Revelations of Divine Love* (Penguin Classics Edition 1966)

Carl Jung, *Man and his Symbols* (Doubleday 1964)

Carl Jung, *Memories, Dreams, Reflections* (Pantheon 1963)

Carl Jung, *The Spirit in Man, Art and Literature* (Routledge 1967)

Robin Karr-Morse and Meredith S Wiley, *Ghosts from the Nursery – Tracing the Roots of Violence* (Atlantic Monthly Books 1997)

Bernardo Kastrup, *Dreamed Up Reality* (John Hunt Publishing 2011)*

Kelsang Gyatso, *Joyful path of Good Fortune* (Tharpa Publications 1995)

Kelsang Gyatso, *The Heart of Wisdom* (Tharpa Publications 1996)

Kelsang Gyatso, *Universal Compassion* (Tharpa Publications 1988)

Kelsang Gyatso, *Meaningful to Behold* (Tharpa Publications 1980)

Kelsang Gyatso, *Essence of Vajrayana* (Tharpa Publications 1997)

Kelsang Gyatso, *The New Guide to Dakini Land* (Tharpa Publications 2013)

Josephine Klein, *Jacob's Ladder* (Taylor & Francis 2003)

Melanie Klein, *Collected works* (Facsimile edition Hogarth Press 1975)

Arthur Koestler, *The Act of Creation* (Hutchinson 1964)

Arthur Koestler, *The Roots of Coincidence* (Hutchinson 1972)

Ray Kurzweil, *How to Create a Mind* (Viking 2012)

David Luke, *Otherworlds* (Muswell Hill Press 2017)

David Luke and Rory Spowers (editors), *DMT Dialogues* (Park Street Press 2018)

Jeffery A Martin, *The Finders* (Integration Press 2019)*

Ignacio Matte Blanco, *The Unconscious as Infinite Sets* (Routledge 1975)*

Ignacio Matte Blanco, *Thinking, Feeling and Being* (Routledge 1988)*

Robert A Monroe, *Journeys out of the Body* (Doubleday 1971)

Jeremy Narby, *The Cosmic Serpent* (Victor Gollancz 1998)

Michael Newton, *Journey of Souls* (Llewellyn Publications 1994)

Michael Newton, *Life Between Lives* (Llewellyn publications 2004)*

James Oroc, *Tryptamine Palace* (Park Street Press 2009)*

Michael Pollan, *How to Change Your Mind* (Allen Lane 2018)

Eric Rayner, *Unconscious Logic* (Routledge 1995)

Robert Rabbin, *The 5 Principles of Authentic Living* (RealTime Speaking 2011)

Robert Rabbin, *The Sacred Hub* (New Leaders Press 1995)

Sogyal Rinpoche, *The Tibetan Book of Living and Dying* (Harper Collins 1992)*

Jane Roberts, *Seth Speaks* (Prentice-Hall 1972)*

Jane Roberts, *The Nature of Personal Identity* (Prentice-Hall 1974)

Jane Roberts, *The "Unknown" Reality Vol1* (Prentice-Hall 1977)

Jane Roberts, *The "Unknown" Reality Vol2* (Prentice-Hall 1979)

Jane Roberts, *Dreams, Evolution and Value Fulfilment Vol1* (Prentice-Hall 1986)

Richard Rudd, *The Gene Keys* (Gene Keys Publishing 2009)*

Richard Rudd, *The Seven Sacred Seals* (Gene Keys Publishing 2016)*

Richard Rudd, *The Art of Contemplation* (Gene Keys Publishing 2018)*

Carla Rueckert, *Living the Law of One* (L/L Research 2009)

Walter Russell, *The Secret of Light* (Walter Russell, NYC 1947)*

Allan Schore, *Affect Regulation and the Origin of Self* (Psychology Press 1994)

Helen Schumann, *The Course in Miracles* (The Foundation for Inner Peace 1975)*

Robert Schwartz, *Your Soul's Plan* (Frog Books 2009)*

Robert Schwartz, *Your Soul's Gift* (Watkins Publishing 2012)*

Rupert Sheldrake, *The Presence of the Past* (Times Books 1988)

Rupert Sheldrake, *The Science Delusion* (Coronet 2012)

Rupert Sheldrake, *Is the Sun Conscious?* (paper published 2021)*

Daniel J Siegel, *The Developing Mind* (Guildford Press 1999)

Daniel J Siegel and Mary Hartzell, *Parenting from the Inside Out* (Penguin 2004)

Valerie Sinason, *Mental Handicap and the Human Condition* (Free Association Books 1992)

Michael Talbot, *The Holographic Universe* (Harper Collins 1991)*

Andy Tomlinson, *Exploring the Eternal Soul* (From the Heart Press 2007)

Nick Totton (editor), *Psychoanalysis and the Paranormal* (Routledge 2003)

Eckhart Tolle, *The Power of Now* (New World Library 1999)

Eckhart Tolle, *A New Earth* (Viking 2005)

James Tunney, *The Mystery of the Trapped Light* (Amazon 2020)

Michael Tymn, *No One Really Dies* (Whitecrow Books 2020)

Neale Donald Walsch, *Conversations with God (Vols1-3)* (Holder and Stoughton 1995-1998)

Neale Donald Walsch, *Conversations with God (Vol4)* (Watkins 2017)

Ken Wilber, *A Brief History of Everything* (Shambhala Publications 1996)

Ken Wilber, *Integral Psychology* (Shambala Publications 1994)

Meg Harris Williams, *The Vale of Soulmaking* (Routledge 2005)

Marc Wittmann, *Altered States of Consciousness* (MIT Press 2018)

Printed in Great Britain
by Amazon

42402984R00155